Studies in International Affairs Number 25

INTERNATIONAL MARINE ENVIRONMENT POLICY: THE ECONOMIC DIMENSION

W9-CLE-371

By Charles S. Pearson

The Washington Center of Foreign Policy Research School of Advanced International Studies The Johns Hopkins University

The Johns Hopkins University Press Baltimore and London

Manufactured in the United States of America.

The Johns Hopkins University Press, Baltimore, Maryland 21218
The Johns Hopkins University Press Ltd., London

Library of Congress Catalog Card Number 74–24793
ISBN 0–8018–1712–9 (clothbound)
ISBN 0–8018–1713–7 (paperback)

Originally published, 1975
Paperbound edition, 1975

Library of Congress Cataloging in Publication data will be found on the last printed page of this book.

INTERNATIONAL MARINE
ENVIRONMENT POLICY

Studies in International Affairs Number 25

To Leilani

CONTENTS

TABLES

FIGURES

PREFACE AND ACKNOWLEDGMENTS

Although this study is concerned with the economic dimension of ocean policy, its intended audience is broader than the economics profession. An effort has been made to present terms, concepts, and arguments so that they are fully accessible to anyone interested in ocean policy formation or the formulation of environmental controls. Additionally, the oceans are the nexus of an intricate international political controversy. To neglect the larger political matrix within which ocean environment decisions are made, and concentrate on narrow economic considerations, would risk missing the essential forces at work. An attempt has been made to have the research current through spring 1974.

I would like to express my gratitude to Dean Robert Osgood, Ann Hollick of the School of Advanced International Studies (SAIS) Ocean Policy Project, and Richard Cooper, who have read the manuscript and have offered helpful suggestions. My graduate student seminar members at SAIS Johns Hopkins and at the College of Marine Studies of the University of Delaware have also made substantial contributions and I thank them collectively. Mary Nolz has done an excellent job of typing, and I am in her debt. Financial support through the SAIS Ocean Policy Project and the National Science Foundation is gratefully acknowledged. Any omissions, inaccuracies, or obscurities that remain are entirely my responsibility.

INTRODUCTION

Two characteristics of the oceans shape their environmental destiny. First, the oceans lie below the continental land masses, and the laws of gravity make them the natural sinks for societies' wastes. Polluted river runoff, sewage outfalls, wastes from routine ocean transport, deliberate ocean dumping, and atmospheric fallout all find their way into ocean space.

Second, the high seas are neither under private ownership nor national jurisdiction. Consequently, without the inherent, if imperfect, protection that accompanies either private ownership or sovereign jurisdiction, they are increasingly used as waste disposal sites. Regulations governing the environmental use of oceans must contend with these central facts.

Environmental control measures to maintain or improve the quality of international environmental resources such as the oceans, therefore, pose special problems not encountered in a domestic setting. While environmental control (EC) measures at the national level can be interpreted as corrections to the system of property rights over domestic resources, the problems of controls are compounded at the international level. Private, national or supra-national ownership rights are absent. Therefore, controls must evolve *pari passu* with international law or from specific agreements among sovereign states rather than from the direct legislative authority of a national government over its own environmental resources. At the same time that international environmental control activities face many of the same questions that arise when formulating domestic environmental control policy, the context in which these questions are resolved is considerably more complicated.

Additionally, the initiation of environmental control policies can have a profound impact on the distribution of welfare among various individuals and groups. Both welfare identification and institutions for compensating for welfare changes, or redistributing welfare, remain far stronger at the national level than at the international level. Consequently, the distributional or equity implications of environmental control measures, which are often neglected domestically in order to concentrate on resource allocation efficiency criteria, cannot be set aside at the international level. The equity consequences of environmental control measures directly affect the well-being of the states that negotiate the environmental control agreements, and therefore must be incorporated in any analysis of international environmental control policy formation.

Finally, analysis of ocean environmental issues, the subject of this study, cannot employ the simple models for examining common property resources which postulate a single use for the resource and market prices for the resource services. The oceans have multiple and conflicting uses, some of which are valuable but unpriced in the market place. Analysis of ocean environment issues must recognize and consider these other uses.

The purpose of this study is to explore the issues involved in efforts to arrest the environmental deterioration of the oceans. The broad perspective will be that of economics, and the discussion will draw on the extensive recent literature concerned with the economics of environmental control. No attempt is made to fully describe the physical characteristics of waste flows into the oceans or their effects on the ocean environment. Rather, the focus is on the contribution that economic reasoning can make toward rational international environmental resource management.

While the insights of economic theory can give only a partial view of the environmental management of the oceans, and despite the added complexity arising from the absence of jurisdiction over ocean space, it is the contention of this study that:

—the economic roots of environmental deterioration and environmental control activities are similar at the national and international level;

—terminology, concepts, and conclusions developed at the domestic level can contribute to understanding the process of environmental control promotion at the international level;
—the effectiveness of ocean environmental control policy can be augmented if due recognition is given to economic considerations.

International law and international conventions regulating the environmental use of oceans are still rudimentary, but are developing rapidly. To anchor the discussion in reality, attention will be given to the recently concluded conventions on ocean dumping, and on the prevention of pollution from ships.[1]

The objectives of the study are best accomplished by dividing the discussion into four major sections.[2] Chapter I provides necessary background information by reviewing the economic interpretation of the environmental crisis, by pointing out the rationale for government intervention in the management of environmental resources, and by setting forth and discussing the important questions that arise in contemplating intervention. Chapter II develops the argument that the same economic forces that have led to environmental controls on the national level are now being brought to bear on international environmental resources, but the different context leads to somewhat different results. Chapter III returns to the economic questions that are posed by government management of environmental resources and evaluates the Ocean Dumping Convention in light of these. Chapter IV does the same for the Prevention of Pollution from Ships Convention. In both Chapters III and IV the often neglected

[1] The Convention on Prevention of Marine Pollution by Dumping of Wastes and Other Matter, 1972, and the International Convention for the Prevention of Pollution from Ships, 1973.

[2] For descriptions of wastes entering the oceans and the effects thereon see, among others, M. Hardy, "International Control of Marine Pollution," *Natural Resources Journal,* 3, no. 2 (April 1971); reports of the Joint Group of Experts on the Scientific Aspects of Marine Pollution (GESAMP), including the report of the fourth session, September 1972, reprinted in *Hearings on the 1973 IMCO Conference on Marine Pollution from Ships Before the Senate Committee on Commerce,* 93rd Cong., 1st Sess. Serial No. 93–52 (1973); International Maritime Consultative Organization (IMCO), Report of Study No. VI, *The Environmental and Financial Consequences of Oil Pollution from Ships*, prepared by the Programmes Analysis Unit of the

but critical issue of the equity consequences of environmental control activities is introduced. Appendix I contains the text of the Ocean Dumping Convention and a summary of the Prevention of Pollution from Ships Convention.

U.K. Department of Trade & Industry (1973) (hereinafter cited as IMCO Study VI); D. Charter and J. Porricelli, "Quantitative Estimates of Petroleum to the Oceans." paper presented at the May 1973 Workshop on Inputs, Fates and Effects of Petroleum in the Marine Environment, National Academy of Sciences, National Research Council; and Council on Environmental Quality, *Ocean Dumping, A National Policy* (Washington, 1970).

Economic analysis of international environmental resource management is not entirely novel. See, for example, A. Scott, "The Economics of International Transmission of Pollution," in OECD, *Problems of Environmental Economics* (Paris, 1971). Also see an important collection of articles by the OECD entitled *Problems in Transfrontier Pollution* (Paris, 1974). Much of the discussion, however, has been from the legal and institutional perspective. See L. Hargrove (ed.), *Law, Institutions and the Global Environment* (Oceania, 1972).

INTERNATIONAL MARINE ENVIRONMENT POLICY

Studies in International Affairs Number 25

I. GOVERNMENT INTERVENTION: RATIONALE AND ISSUES

RATIONALE: MARKET FAILURE

The now widely accepted economic interpretation of the problem of environmental deterioration starts from the observation that certain environmental resources, such as airsheds and water courses, have positive economic value as inputs into production processes, as directly consumed, as for example in recreational activities, or as disposal mediums into which wastes from production and consumption activities can be discharged. At the same time, these services of environmental resources do not generally command market prices. Without prices there is little incentive to either allocate the resources to their most productive uses or to conserve them. In short, by not attaching prices to environmental resource services, the market system fails to achieve efficient resource allocations.[1]

The failure of market prices to develop for environmental resources can be traced in part to an earlier time in which they were in excess supply. Resources in excess supply will have neither an economic (scarcity) value nor be able to command a market price. As ownership is worthless, the resources are either not owned, or are owned by the society as a whole as common property resources. In such circumstances a zero market price is entirely consistent with efficient resource allocation.

Over time, however, increasing demands for environmen-

---

[1] Evidence indicates that environmental resources also have been systematically undervalued in nonmarket economies, and that they have not experienced appreciably better environmental protection. See M. Goldman, "The Convergence of Environmental Disruption," *Science* 170 (Oct. 2, 1970).

tal resources as inputs into production (e.g., industrial water use), for direct consumption (e.g., water recreation), and particularly for waste disposal have eroded the basis for excess supply and they have become economically scarce.[2] The traditions of excess supply coupled with technical difficulties in appropriating environmental resources to private ownership precluded property rights, and hence markets from emerging. That is, air, and to a lesser extent water, resources present formidable difficulties in demarcating boundaries and enforcing exclusion of nonowners.

Without market prices for the use of environmental services in production, the private (market) prices of goods and services do not reflect the full social costs of production. The discrepancy between private (market) prices for goods and services and their social costs means inefficiency in resource allocation decisions. More specifically, under-pricing products which place relatively high demands on environmental services results in levels of production and consumption which are excessive. Environmental resources are not allocated to competing uses on the basis of highest productivity, but are used and abused as dumping grounds for waste disposal. There is no economic incentive to reduce waste loads through treatment, recycling, or process modification. Although there appears to be a clear case for government intervention to correct the failures of the marketplace and improve social welfare, we shall see that it is not always the case.

An alternative way of explaining market failure associated with common property resources uses the economic concepts of optimality and externalities.[3] A particular allocation of resources is said to be optimal if it is impossible to reallocate them so that one individual or group's welfare is improved

[2] The spatial dimension of economic activity and environmental resources should not be neglected. Excess supplies will coexist in time, with economic scarcities depending on the spatial configuration of production and consumption activities and resources.

[3] For a clear and stimulating discussion of these concepts, see E. Mishan, "The Postwar Literature on Externalities: An Interpretive Essay," *Journal of Economic Literature*, 9, no. 1 (March 1971).

without necessarily harming the welfare of others.[4] Stated conversely, a particular allocation of resources is less than optimal if it can be rearranged so that no individual need suffer a welfare loss and at least one individual is made better off. Familiar examples of suboptimal situations are found when national tariffs distort the free flow of trade and limit the full exploitation of comparative advantage, or when monopoly power restricts output and raises prices.

It is important to note that optimum resource allocation has customarily been analyzed separately from distributional or equity considerations. Moving from a suboptimal to an optimal position will have welfare distributional consequences. One cannot say, a priori, which situation is more desirable from the viewpoint of equity, and unless the welfare consequences of the change are fully compensated it is difficult to assert that total welfare has necessarily increased. A change in the tariff law, even if it increases total output and income, will harm some. Unless they are fully compensated, it is difficult to assert that total welfare has increased. This proposition carries special force in discussions of ocean resource questions, for institutions for redistributing welfare internationally, or granting compensation to damaged parties, are rudimentary at best.

In a market system prices play the dual role of guiding consumption and production decisions. It can be shown that one of the conditions necessary to achieve optimum resource allocation is that market prices be equal to the full marginal social costs of production, including the costs to society of using environmental resource services. But we have seen that a central feature of common property resources that have an economic, or scarcity, value is that the users of the resource services do not have to pay a price. Despite their economic value they are considered "free goods." Accordingly, a divergence between the social costs of the activity and the private costs to individuals and firms occurs, and prices fail to reflect all social costs.

---

[4] The technical term is "pareto optimality."

Users of the environmental resource for waste disposal purposes create costs that are external to themselves but are borne by others and are called externalities or external diseconomies.[5] It is the existence of externalities that drives the wedge between private and social costs. Although externalities are not confined to environmental deterioration, some familiar examples from this literature illustrate the concept. If an upstream petrochemical firm discharges toxic wastes into a river that is a common property resource and produces a downstream fish kill, then the costs of the fish kill are external to the firm, but are direct costs to others. In similar fashion, uncontrolled automobile emissions damage the health of urban residents, and overhead transmission lines reduce scenic qualities and produce amenity losses. In each of these examples the costs that are external to one party— the petrochemical firm, the commuter, the power company—are absorbed elsewhere in society. If the externality is left uncontrolled there is no incentive present for output reduction, waste treatment, recycling, or process modification. Again, the rationale is established for government intervention in the management of environmental resources to improve allocational efficiency and the social welfare.

Certain limitations should be mentioned on the potential for government intervention to improve the social welfare, however. First, there may be substantial costs involved in collecting information on the damages from externalities and control costs, in formulating environmental control regulations, and in enforcing these regulations. These costs must be

---

[5] Externalities are defined in the literature as the direct (nonmarket) imposition of costs or benefits on one economic agent as the incidental result of the activities of another economic agent. External diseconomies deal with costs; external economies deal with benefits. Note that externalities can flow among consumers (smoking in a confined place), among producers (upstream chemical wastes harming downstream commercial fisheries), from producers to consumers and from consumers to producers. The term "incidental" in the definition might be misleading. It means that the *purpose* of activity generating the externality is not the externality itself. However, the externality may well be fully anticipated and is not accidental.

subtracted from the potential improvement in social welfare arising from improved allocative efficiency. Second, as noted earlier, moving from one state of environmental quality to another will necessarily have welfare distributional consequences, and unless all are compensated for losses it is difficult to assert that social welfare has indeed improved. Finally, a proposition in economic theory entitled "The Theory of Second Best" demonstrates that if two or more distortions in the economy exist (from externalities or otherwise), removing one distortion through government intervention need not always move the economy toward a more optimal position. While these factors place limits on government intervention, they do not eliminate the rationale.

Before turning to the criterion for government intervention suggested by the preceding analysis, it is useful to make two additional points. First, pollution-related external diseconomies have the characteristic that the external cost, or welfare loss, always flows from that group that uses the environment for waste disposal to other users of the environment. Accordingly, when there are no restrictions and multiple uses of environmental common property resources, implicit rights to the resources are invariably awarded to the polluters.

Second, the question arises why private transactions between the polluter and the damaged parties do not arise, such that, through bargaining, an optimum allocation of resources obtains without requiring government intervention. Taking a simple example, if individual A perceives a threat to his welfare from the proposed construction of a building by B which will block off A's scenic view, and if the existing law is such that B has a legal right to build, can we rely on A to either purchase the adjoining property or buy a scenic easement from B? If the potential loss to A is greater than the potential gain to B, would not A be able to offer a "bribe" to B sufficient to prevent the construction of the building? If, in contrast, the value of the view to A is less than the potential value of the building to B, the bribe offer will fail, but presumably resources would be optimally allocated despite the welfare loss to A.[6] Indeed, in this example, in which the source of the potential welfare loss is easy to identify and market channels for expressing preferences in monetary terms are well developed, there may not be a case for government intervention to supersede private transactions.

This example is instructive for it highlights the welfare consequences of a particular legal regime. If the law gave rights to A over B, the monetary payment would flow in the opposite direction. B could offer to buy out A or pay him compensation for the loss of scenic amenities. The welfare distribution consequences would be different. Whether ultimate resource allocation (building or not) would be the same in the two legal regimes is more difficult to determine. The very important Coase Theorem states that if transactions costs are zero the allocative results are independent of the assignment of rights. Mishan, however, points out that the change in welfare accompanying the change in the legal regime can alter both A's valuation of the scenic view and B's ability to offer compensation. In any event, we should note that the law may be written to discourage private transaction—i.e., prohibit A from accepting compensation— and thus prevent attaining optimal resource allocation.

In many cases of environmental diseconomies, however, the number of damaged parties is large, the physical pathways through which the diseconomies are transmitted are complex, and the sources of the pollution are difficult to identify. When transactions costs are high—aggregating the interests of the many who are damaged, identifying and negotiating with polluters, enforcing contracts and preventing freeloaders—private bargaining fails and the rationale for government intervention reemerges.

---

[6]See R. Coase. "The Problem of Social Cost"; J. Dales. "Land, Water & Ownership"; and G. Calabresi, "Transactions Cost, Resource Allocation, and Liability Rules," all reprinted in Dorfman and Dorfman (eds.). *Economics of the Environment* (Norton, 1972). Note that possible defensive action by A, moving to another location, might be the least expensive alternative, providing that the value of his original residence is not too greatly reduced.

Two major conclusions concerning environmental control policies for the correction of external diseconomies can be drawn from the preceding discussion. These conclusions will be relevant to the analysis of ocean environmental control policy. First, to overcome the inefficiencies associated with common property resources and externalities, control policies must be formulated so that the external costs are internalized. Whether this objective is best served by extending private property rights to common property resources, by facilitating the negotiation of private arrangements among users, or by explicit government regulations or charges governing the use of environmental resources, depends on particular circumstances. In all cases, however, it will be desirable to bring the costs of environmental resources within the calculus of users.

Second, the process of correcting the misallocations associated with externalities will effect the welfare of various groups differently. Specifically, the imposition of environmental regulations concerning the use of common property resources will revoke the prior implicit rights of waste dischargers and reduce their welfare.[7] These rights will be awarded to others whose welfare will increase. The rearrangement of rights to economically valuable resources and the implied changes in welfare deserve study in themselves. What is equally important is that they affect the process by which environmental control policy is formulated.

ECONOMIC CRITERIA FOR EVALUATING ENVIRONMENTAL CONTROL POLICY

Recognizing that the extension of private property rights over most environmental resources is precluded by difficulties in appropriating to private ownership and would be resisted on the grounds that too much power over essential resources would be vested in private hands, and further observing that even if it were done the transactions costs

---

[7] Unless previously disposal was associated with zero economic cost.

associated with private bargaining among resource users would be prohibitive, the case for government intervention becomes persuasive to control growing externalities and arrest a deteriorating environment and levels of welfare. In contemplating intervention the government must make choices in three critical areas and, in turn, these offer criteria for an economic evaluation of the policies. By examining these three areas for decision we will also establish a framework for examining environmental controls over ocean resources.

Decisions must be made on the following questions:

—the types and amounts of pollution to be permitted or, alternatively, the extent of pollution abatement activity;
—the most appropriate instruments for the government to employ to obtain environmental quality objectives;
—whether the distribution of costs and benefits resulting from the environmental control measures is acceptable, or whether compensatory action should be taken.

These three areas for decision are clearly interrelated. A decision to seek zero levels of a particular pollutant suggests total prohibition by law as the most logical instrument. At the same time the transition costs of moving to alternative inputs or processes can be reduced by staging the prohibition over time. An example of this is the phase out of the use of DDT in the United States. Alternatively, it may be decided that full prohibition would not be desirable, but the choice of the control instrument—say using the tax system to induce compliance as opposed to effluent standards plus government subsidies—would influence the distribution of environmental control costs. What is essential for the purposes of this study is that each area for decision contains an economic dimension from which a criterion for evaluation can be extracted.

Establishing Environmental Quality Goals

In selecting environmental quality goals, the guiding economic principle for optimal allocation of resources is that they should be allocated so that the incremental, or marginal, social productivity of the resource in each use is equalized.

That is, as a general principle, a resource should be allocated among competing uses in such a manner that the social product from the last unit of that resource is of equal value in all use categories. For environmental resources, such as a river or other body of water, which are used as inputs into production (industrial cooling), which are directly consumed (as for example through municipal drinking water), and which are used for waste disposal, the principle implies that the correct opportunity cost for assessing the waste disposal services of the river is the value of the other services foregone—as an industrial coolant or as potable water.

The marginal costs of abatement are the real resource costs (labor, capital, intermediate inputs, etc.) used to reduce the last unit of pollution; the marginal social benefits are the damages avoided by withholding the last unit of pollution. It is immediately evident that a zero pollution policy is uneconomic except in the (rare) instances when the cost of reducing the last unit of pollution is less than the benefit derived from eliminating that unit. Both logic and empirical studies show that, generally, as pollution abatement approaches 100%, the incremental cost of abatement rises and the incremental benefit, or damages avoided, falls. Thus, in the normal case, the optimum level of pollution abatement is something less than 100%, and indeed that level is reached before the point at which total abatement costs equal total benefits.

The point can be made more graphic. Consider the following simple diagram. The horizontal axis measures the extent of abatement up to 100%. The vertical axis measures both abatement costs and benefits (damages avoided). Curve C represents abatement costs and B abatement benefits. Abatement of 100% would have costs in excess of benefits and would be uneconomic. Choosing the environmental quality goal associated with Q, where total benefits and costs are equalized, would also be inefficient. Net welfare is greatest at G, where the marginal benefit represented by the slope of the benefit function is just equal to marginal costs represented by the slope of the cost function.

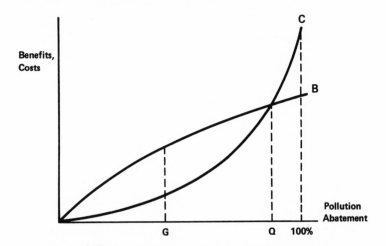

Fig. 1. Benefits, Cost—Pollution Abatement

The difficulties in translating this principle into specific pollution abatement objectives and implementing these objectives through environmental control measures should not be minimized. It is generally felt that benefit functions (damage functions) are more difficult to estimate than are cost functions. Benefit functions are particularly sticky because the scientific data for evaluating the ecological effects of pollutants is often spotty or inconclusive, and because a significant portion of environmental services do not pass through markets, complicating the task of valuing damages avoided. Also important is the transmutability of pollutants—an environmental control measure, such as controlling ocean dumping of sewage sludge, which results in greater atmospheric pollution from incineration merely shifts the damages from one environmental medium to another.

If complete data are available, the appropriate analytical technique for selecting environmental quality goals is benefit cost. Unfortunately, however, many of the benefits from pollution abatement, such as recreational services, esthetic amenities, wilderness experience, and so forth, do not pass through markets and cannot be valued using market prices.

Too often benefit cost analyses are partial, excluding non-market costs and benefits, and therefore lead to erroneous decisions. Proxy estimation techniques of benefits, such as "willingness to pay," can sometimes be employed, but they have inherent limitations. An alternative is to include all benefits and costs that can be given a monetary value in the analysis, compute the excess of benefits over costs, and then pose the question: Are the unvalued environmental damages of a certain action likely to be greater or less than this net benefit? While still subjective, this alternative does not require an exact value to be placed on environmental damage (or abatement benefit), but allows for a simple greater-or-less-than decision. Finally, if benefits cannot be known, a widely used technique is cost-effectiveness. This method simply takes as a given the desirability of pollution abatement and evaluates alternative abatement techniques on the basis of cost per physical unit of pollution avoided. The use of these techniques for marine pollution abatement is explored in Chapters III and IV.

Selecting Environmental Control Instruments

Having established environmental quality goals or, implicitly, having selected pollution abatement objectives, either according to the marginal principle outlined above or by some other method, the next area for government decision is the choice of instruments for attaining these objectives. The actual selection will depend on many factors, including the nature and characteristics of the pollutant, the political pressures brought to bear by interest groups, and the customary instruments employed by the government to achieve other social policy goals.

The relevant economic criterion for choice is that instrument or set of instruments that will minimize the real resource costs of achieving the objectives. Economists, no less than others, recognize that policy formation is a disorderly and often inefficient process, and they accept the fact that the adoption of an idealized efficient policy is a remote possibility. Nevertheless, it is their function to identify and make explicit, to the extent possible, the real resource costs of using alternative policy instruments for social purposes. With regard to environmental control policy, four considerations become important:

—noting which instruments will have the effect of internalizing external costs and correcting the distortions of market prices;
—determining which instruments will minimize enforcement costs;
—identifying which instruments will provide the greatest encouragement to innovation in pollution abatement technology, and hence reduce future costs;
—deciding which instruments will most easily distinguish between high and low abatement cost pollution sources, so that overall abatement costs are minimized.[8]

Regarding the first point, internalizing externalities, there is general agreement that in principle the costs of pollution abatement should be borne by those who pollute or, in the case of pollution occurring in the production process, by the consumers of the products through higher prices. This principle stands in opposition to financing pollution abatement costs out of general tax revenues, which would permit continued price distortion.[9] It should be emphasized that while this principle has rhetorical support both in the United States and elsewhere, there exist a number of channels through which the U.S. government is now picking up a portion of the abatement costs in the private sector. These include special amortization allowances for abatement equipment which is a tax subsidy, tax-free pollution abatement bond financing, and provision of municipal waste treatment facilities to industry at less than full cost.

An interesting debate on the question of domestic en-

---

[8] For a more extensive discussion of alternative environmental control measures see A. Kneese and B. Bower, "Standards, Charges & Equity," in *Managing Water Quality: Economics, Technology, Institutions:* (The Johns Hopkins Press, 1968); Dales, "Land, Water, and Ownership"; and Council on Environmental Quality *Second Annual Report* (1971).

[9] The popular but misleading term is "polluter-pays-principle." It is misleading because in production pollution the producer is free to pass on abatement costs to consumers and because the producer is not made responsible for any residual damages after abatement objectives have been met.

vironmental control instruments has been in progress and, as the issues are directly relevant to ocean environmental control measures, it is useful to sketch in the main points. Restricting the discussion to these measures that keep private sector abatement costs in the private sector, one can distinguish between two broad groups—direct regulation of polluters through effluent and emission standards, and indirect measures which work through the price system and offer financial incentives to either encourage or discourage certain activities. Within the latter group are effluent/emission tax schemes, subsidy payments tied to pollution abatement, and "environmental usage certificate" schemes. The first would place a tax on emissions, forcing the polluter to consider social costs, and would provide a financial incentive to reduce waste loads. The second would create an opportunity cost for continued pollution in the form of a subsidy foregone and would also provide a financial incentive to reduce waste loads. The environmental usage certificate schemes would create artificial markets for environmental resources and as competing users bid for "rights" to use the environment, prices would be established and again there would be incentive to reduce waste loads.

Both groups of control instruments can be constructed so that the external costs associated with production are internalized—a condition which was earlier argued necessary for optimal resource allocation. Provided certain conditions were met, both groups could achieve particular environmental objectives at the least social cost.

Proponents of instruments that use the price system point out, however, that in the case of regulations and standards the informational requirements placed on the government regulatory agency are enormous and very expensive to collect. It can be shown that if polluters differ as to either their individual waste-treatment cost functions, or as to their prospects for recycling wastes, or as to their ability to reduce waste loads through product or process changes, then to achieve least cost pollution abatement it is essential to distinguish among polluters, obliging those facing lower clean-up costs to shoulder a larger abatement burden and permitting high abatement cost polluters to engage in less clean-up.[10] The results would permit greater abatement at the same resource cost or lower resource costs for the same abatement objective. While it is theoretically possible to make these distinctions among polluters using the standards/ regulations approach, the regulatory agency would need full knowledge of all individual abatement cost functions, and the expense of acquiring this information might be prohibitive. In contrast, it is argued, reliance on the price system would relieve the government of this information requirement and permit each polluter to decide, on the basis of his own costs, whether it would be less expensive to reduce pollution levels and avoid an emissions tax or to pay the tax and not incur emissions charges.[11]

A simple example illustrates this point. Assume the per unit cost of reducing a particular pollutant were $8 and $12 respectively for source A and source B. Assume also that A initially generates 50 units and B generates 50 units of the pollutant and that the regulatory authority has determined, on the basis of the marginal cost/benefit principle discussed earlier, that the total emissions of the pollutant should be no more than 50 units. If, under a standards/regulatory system, each source is ordered to cut its effluent level by 50%, the abatement cost will be $500. If, however, a tax on effluents were set at $10 per unit, source A would find it less expensive to eliminate them, while source B would find it less expensive to pay the effluent charge. The abatement goal of 50% reduction is met at a real resource cost of $400.[12]

[10] The formal requirement would state that the marginal abatement costs must be equalized for all polluters. Application of this principle may encounter opposition on equity grounds.

[11] In either event, the scheme would increase production costs and presumably product prices, thus closing the gap between private and social costs. While all three methods which rely on the price system would automatically distinguish among polluters on the basis of abatement cost functions, there are significant differences among them. See CEQ *Second Annual Report*.

[12] The example is unrealistic in that constant abatement costs are assumed. Source B would have a financial cost of $500, but as this is an effluent tax payment it represents a welfare transfer rather than a real resource cost.

In addition to its ability to automatically distinguish between high and low abatement cost polluters, an effluent tax scheme has the additional advantage of acting as a continuing incentive to reduce pollution. Once a polluter has met a specific effluent standard he has no incentive to go beyond, while a tax would offer continuing incentive for further abatement.

The question of the efficiency of the instruments, then, provides a second economic criterion for evaluation of environmental control policy.

Environmental Control Welfare Consequences

Whatever instruments are selected to achieve the desired environmental goal, the next decision the government must face is whether or not the resulting change in the distribution of welfare should be modified. Any environmental control measure, be it a prohibition on the use of DDT or a disposal tax on automobiles, will confer benefits on certain groups and costs on other groups.[13] For example, banning the hormone DES will ultimately increase prices at the meat counter. Regulations limiting the use of high sulphur fuel increase the price of electricity. Shifting air flights to outlying areas to minimize noise levels in urban areas results in higher business commuting costs (including travel time). The beneficiaries of the action may coincide closely with those who bear the costs (DES), or they may be a quite distinct group (urban non-air travelers). In all cases the environmental control measure involves a reassignment of rights over environmental resources and thus a welfare transfer.

There has been very little effort to systematically examine the equity consequences of environmental measures and, apart from efforts to minimize transitional costs such as temporary job losses through plant closings, almost no attempt to institute compensatory policy. There is now underway research on the economic impact of water and air pollution legislation on industry profits, competitive position,

[13] If the measure produces an improvement in allocative efficiency those who benefit could fully compensate those who suffer welfare losses and still be better off.

employment, and so forth, but the emphasis has been on the transitory costs of moving from one environmental "state" to another, rather than on the ultimate redistribution of welfare that accompanies these measures.

The neglect of environmental control-induced welfare charges on the domestic level can be explained on two grounds. First, there is a long tradition among economists to separate out resource allocation questions from welfare distribution issues, to classify distribution as essentially a political issue outside the narrower interests of economics, and to rely on domestic institutions, such as the tax system, to achieve the particular welfare distribution pattern that society wishes.

Second, there is a widespread and deeply held feeling throughout the community that, beyond some minimal levels that have been far exceeded, the "right" to use environmental resources for waste disposal should yield to the rights of other users—that is, past this minimum level, the right to clean air and water for health, for recreation, and for esthetic enjoyment takes precedence. This view carries with it a rejection of the past environmental resource rights distribution and an implied endorsement of the post-environmental control distribution. Consequently, no compensatory policy would be needed.

Whatever the merits of these explanations for the domestic neglect, the situation is critically altered in the context of international environmental resources. International environmental control measures cannot be handed down from a body with ultimate jurisdiction over the resources, for there is no such supra-national body, but must be painfully built up through negotiations among sovereign states. Because welfare identification remains strongest on the national level, and because the institutions for redistributing welfare internationally are rudimentary, the distribution of environmental control costs and benefits becomes an integral part of the environmental control negotiations themselves.[14]

[14] This point is strongly emphasized by Christy when discussing the control of ocean fish stocks. See F. Christy, "Fisheries: Common Property,

SUMMARY

To summarize the argument thus far, if left unregulated the external diseconomies associated with using environmental resources for waste disposal will create a split between private and social costs. In such circumstances the market system fails to allocate resources in the most efficient (optimum) fashion and presents an opportunity for government intervention to improve the social welfare. In contemplating intervention, the government faces decisions in three areas. With regard to the degree of pollution abatement, the guiding economic principle is to equate the marginal social costs of abatement to the marginal social benefits. With regard to the intervention instruments, there is a strong economic case for using tools that force the internalization of previously external costs, thus reducing the split between private and social costs. Beyond this, an argument can be made for using instruments that work through the price system, such as effluent taxes and environmental usage certificate schemes, when feasible from an enforcement standpoint and when the information costs would be high for the government regulatory agency. With regard to the welfare distribution consequences which inevitably accompany environmental control measures, there has been considerable neglect at the domestic level. Such neglect is not permissible at the international level, for distribution is an essential element in the negotiation of environmental control measures.

Open Access, and the Common Heritage," chapter 6, *Pacem in Maribus* (Royal University of Malta Press, 1971), Vol. II, reprinted by Resources for the Future, Reprint 101.

INTERPRETING OCEAN ENVIRONMENT CONTROLS

THE THESIS

In an exceptionally interesting attempt to integrate economic theory with the development of property rights, Demsetz has argued that "a primary function of property rights is guiding incentives to achieve a greater internalization of externalities," and that "property rights develop to internalize externalities when the gains from internalization become larger than the costs of internalization."[1] He suggests, then, an economic interpretation of the development of property rights that rests centrally on correcting the market failure feature of common property resources that was discussed earlier.

While Demsetz was primarily concerned with the process leading to the extension of private property rights over land, and although his seminal paper was not directly concerned with environmental externalities, we contend in this study that the same economic forces that in some instances impel the extension of private property rights result, in the case of environmental resources, in the extension of government regulations limiting their use. Furthermore, we argue that these same economic forces are now at work in the area of international environmental resources. The current and recent multilateral efforts to regulate ocean resources use can be viewed in part as attempts at "guiding incentives to achieve greater internalization of externalities" that are now being undertaken as "the gains of internalization become larger than the costs of internalization." The absence of national jurisdiction over ocean space has complicated and,

---

[1] H. Demsetz, "Toward a Theory of Property Rights," *American Economic Association Papers & Proceedings* 57, no. 2 (May 1967).

at times, frustrated these attempts. Additionally, other motives are present and have obscured this process. Nevertheless, we feel that viewing the formulation of ocean environment controls from this perspective can offer considerable insight into policy formation and, indeed, contributes to the understanding of nonenvironmental ocean policy formation.

The thesis as originally presented by Demsetz goes beyond a description of the externalities and inefficiencies associated with common property resources. It asserts that the motive force for a change in property rights from common property and free access to private property, with restrictive access through the right of exclusion, is the economic drive for improving resource allocational efficiency. It further argues that, over time, the dynamics of technological change, the opening of new markets and consequent increases in demand, and growing congestion costs, have combined to result in increasing the gains from internalizing externalities. Accordingly, the old property rights regime of free access becomes increasingly inefficient, and resources are continually brought to the point at which the efficiency gains from internalizing externalities exceed the costs of internalization. At that point the prevailing property rights system gives way to more efficient patterns.

An example given by Demsetz is illuminating. Presenting evidence that there was a close relationship between private hunting rights and commercial fur trade among certain groups of Canadian Indians, he observes that before commercial fur trade arose total hunting of fur-bearing animals was limited to personal needs. Consequently, the level of externalities was low, as a successful hunt by one tribe member did not appreciably reduce the yield to others. The prevailing land ownership system was common property, free access, and this was consistent with efficient resource allocation so long as excess supply of fur-bearing animals existed. With the introduction of commercial trade in furs, however, the value of furs and the scale of hunting activity increased. Had there been no change in hunting rights the private costs of a successful hunt would not have included the direct costs imposed on others through reduced yields. Private costs would understate social costs. As each tribe member would have based his decision on private cost calculus, serious over-hunting and depletion of stocks would have resulted, with welfare loss to all.[2]

The increased level of externalities, however, led to the demarcation of private hunting territories and (limited) private land property rights. If land parcels are sufficiently large and the migratory characteristics of the animals sufficiently limited, much of the externality from over-hunting is internalized to the individual, and it becomes economic to exercise restraint in hunting activity. Demsetz notes that there are costs associated with moving to the new property rights system, mainly, enforcement against poaching, but the limited migratory nature of fur-bearing animals in the Northeast has reduced these costs accordingly. In contrast, he observes, the great spatial mobility of game animals in the American Southwest increased enforcement costs and precluded the development of private hunting territories.

As was observed earlier, environmental resources, such as the air mantle and many water resources, are ill-suited to private ownership. Such ownership would carry with it the right to exclude others, and the difficulties of enforcing exclusion and appropriating to private use would be immense. Further, the spatially mobile nature of most pollutants would require resource parcels of very considerable size if externalities were to be internalized. Private ownership, then, would potentially vest enormous wealth in limited numbers of persons and pose serious equity problems for society. As might be expected, therefore, such internalization of environmental externalities that has come about has been through the extension of government control over their use rather than through the development of private property rights. It should be noted that in doing so governments have deliberately revoked or modified the prior implicit rights of

[2] Compare this example to the now widely recognized situation of overgrazing pasture lands owned in common. See Hardin, "The Tragedy of the Commons," *Science* 162 (Dec. 13, 1968).

those who use environmental resources for waste disposal. Environmental control policies are again seen to have an equity or welfare dimension as well as an allocative efficiency dimension.

In modifying the original thesis to account for the need for government regulation of environmental resources rather than private property rights, the argument can be pushed somewhat further. For example, Krier and Montgomery have first proposed that "institutions to more efficiently allocate resources tend to develop in response to relatively increasing value of the resources, whether caused by increasing demand or otherwise," and second, that "as governmentally allocated resources increase in relative value, government intervention tends to evolve toward forms that economize information costs."[3] That is, as intervention proceeds the instruments employed are increasingly chosen on efficiency grounds to minimize the general costs described earlier—enforcement and distinguishing between high and low abatement cost sources of pollution—and to spur technological advances in abatement itself.

In the context of ocean resources, the modified thesis presents a series of propositions that can be evaluated in light of actual ocean resource policy developments. Specifically, a demonstration of the full thesis requires examining four sequential elements:

—the historical property rights regime, while once appropriate, does not now inhibit activities that create external diseconomies;
—the relative value of ocean resource services, and hence the costs associated with external diseconomies, has been increasing;
—the international response has been to develop a system of user rights that either forces the internalization of previously external costs, or curtails the activities that give rise to these costs;
—the techniques for intervening and limiting rights to ocean resources have evolved toward those that minimize information costs and maximize the efficiency of the instruments themselves.

[3] J. Krier and W. D. Montgomery, "Resource Allocation, Information Cost and the Form of Government Intervention," *Natural Resources Journal* 13, no. 1 (January 1973).

Before marshaling evidence to support this set of propositions, we wish to stress several factors that preclude incontrovertible demonstration. First the absence of ultimate sovereignty over the oceans has frustrated and slowed the process. There is no international body that takes a global welfare perspective and that has the authority to regulate ocean resources use accordingly. At the same time, the institutions and channels for compensatory policy to offset or moderate the welfare consequences of ocean environment policy are either rudimentary or nonexistent, and this has further slowed the process. Second, there remains great uncertainty about the environmental effects of waste disposal in ocean space, about resulting economic damages, and about the efficiency of alternative control policies. Even in the more highly developed domestic arena we are still groping for efficient environmental control instruments. With such uncertainty an unambiguous demonstration of these propositions is not expected.

Perhaps most importantly, the process now underway, of drawing away from a regime characterized by freedom of the high seas and free access to the resources therein, and replacing this by simultaneously extending states rights over ocean resources in fisheries and offshore oil and gas production and restricting the use of the oceans for waste disposal, is not solely motivated by the desire to reduce inefficiencies associated with externalities. In addition, states wish to bring under national control the newly created wealth of the oceans. In this fashion the issue of allocative efficiency is joined with a wealth appropriation motive.

The explanation for the "sea change" in ocean ownership patterns now in progress rests centrally on the increased wealth or value of ocean resources. The increase in wealth encourages countries to lay claims to and bring the wealth within national control, at the same time that the increased value of ocean resources is forcing up the inefficiency costs associated with the earlier legal regime. The extension of some national rights and the implicit or explicit limitation of certain other rights reflects both attempts to appropriate new wealth and to mitigate the rising costs of externalities as-sociated with ocean resource use.

The first has been the more customary mode for viewing international political maneuvering over law-of-the-sea is-sues. Traditional analysis has centered on the interplay between the interests of local and distant water fishing countries, continental shelf extensive and shelf-locked coun-tries, land-based mineral producers vs. nations with technological capabilities for developing manganese nodules, and so forth, all within the context set by naval and maritime transport interests.

This perspective, which is basically a wealth distribution viewpoint, has considerable validity overall and especially in relation to specific resources such as offshore petroleum and manganese nodule production. At the same time the second perspective, of control efforts to cope with rising inefficiency costs, complements and extends more traditional analysis. Enough evidence can be presented to provide an illuminating adjunct interpretation of ocean policy formation, particularly concerning ocean environment, and to give some basis for reasoned speculation of future developments.

THE THESIS PARTIALLY DEMONSTRATED

While the central focus of this study is on the environmen-tal use of ocean resources, two considerations require us to take a broader look at ocean resources as we investigate the propositions developed in the preceding discussion. First, an important cause of ocean environment degradation has been the growth in other uses of the ocean with incidental en-vironmental damage. Therefore, the environmental degrada-tion and control problem cannot be disassociated from other ocean resource uses. Second, one can see for other ocean resource uses, and particularly for fisheries, policies and policy proposals that parallel and reinforce the explanation for the development of environmental controls presented here. That is, international controls over ocean resources, such as fisheries, provide an illuminating counterpoint to ocean environment controls.

Concerning the first point to be demonstrated, there can be little question that traditional international law governing ocean resources—freedom of transit on the high seas, free access to fisheries, and the right of capture of fish stocks—does little to inhibit externalities. Whether or not one accepts the distinction between the waters of the high seas, which belong to everyone, or *res communis*, and seabed resources, which belong to no one, or *res nullius*, the central feature of the international law of the oceans until quite recently has been a minimum of restrictions on ocean resource users.

So long as the supplies of ocean resource services, mainly marine transport and fisheries, were in excess of economic demands placed upon them, traditional law was consistent with efficient resource allocation, and the level of externalities was trivial.[4]

The notion of excess supplies was clearly brought out by Grotius, the "father" of the freedom-of-the-seas doctrine, "The vagrant waters of the sea are . . . necessarily free. The right of occupation rests upon the fact that most things become exhausted by promiscuous use and that appropriation consequently is the condition of their utility to human beings. But this is not the case with the sea; it can be exhausted neither by navigation nor by fishing, that is to say, neither of the two ways which it can be used."[5]

While Grotius recognized and discounted the potential flaw of common property ownership—promiscuous use—and clearly stated the rationale for free access as excess supply, the situation has changed. Following Demsetz, the dynamics of technological change, opening of new markets, and grow-

[4] Military security is deliberately excluded as an economic service provided by oceans, although the author is aware of its importance in formulating oceans policy. The interesting point, explored on page 62 below, is the attempt to create ocean zones according to use—military, fisheries, environment—and thus separate users' rights according to function.

[5] Quoted by L. H. J. Legault, "The Freedom of the Seas: License to Pollute?" *University of Toronto Law Journal* 21, no. 2 (1971).

ing congestion costs have eroded the basis for excess supply. Older uses of the oceans have intensified and new uses have evolved.

Specifically, in addition to sustained growth in ocean transport and increased fishing activity, the oceans and seabeds are now extensively used for petroleum production, recreation, and direct waste disposal. Hard mineral production, using manganese nodules, is on the brink of commercial operation. Some background data on the magnitude and economic value of these services is provided in the following tables.

Table 1 provides some information on fish catches by country and year. The world total increased quite steadily and rapidly throughout the sixties, reaching a plateau in 1968–69, with a major drop in 1972. The most rapid increase from 1964 to 1971 was by the USSR, reflecting its growing distant water fleet. Table 2 presents data on the growth of ocean transport services. Total seaborne cargo increased from 550 million metric tons in 1950 to 2,570 million tons in 1970, with oil accounting for an increased proportion. The final column shows that the world's tanker fleet, measured in deadweight tons, increased almost fivefold from 1955 to 1973, from 41 to 201 million d.w.t. Table 3 demonstrates the increased importance of offshore petroleum from 1960 to 1967 and projected increase to 1980. Offshore oil and gas have and will increase absolutely and relative to onshore production. Table 4 illustrates the growing importance of recreational services provided by the oceans.

While no comprehensive estimates of the value of oceans for waste disposal have been made, Figure 2 and Table 5 provide some indications of current use and projections for ocean dumping and oil entering the marine environment. Figure 2 shows the increase in ocean dumping by the United States from 1951 to 1968, by coast. It should be noted that the unit of measure is tons, with dredge spoils dominating the movement, and this is not a particularly useful indicator of ocean pollution potential. Table 5A presents data on 1968 United States dumping by coast and material dumped. Table

TABLE 1. WORLD FISH CATCH BY REGION AND YEAR (thousands metric tons)

	1938	1948	1960	1964	1965	1966	1967	1968	1969	1970	1971	1972	% inc. 1948–72	% inc. 1964–71
World total	21,000	19,600	40,200	51,910	53,200	57,300	60,400	63,900	62,600	69,600	69,400	65,600	210	33
Africa				3,120	3,170	3,350	3,790	4,240	4,260	4,080	3,750			21
North & Central America				4,290	4,450	4,440	4,380	4,640	4,530	4,870	5,010			16
South America				11,260	9,190	11,130	12,200	13,010	11,330	14,850	12,880			14
Asia				18,860	20,250	21,260	22,030	23,850	24,460	26,380	28,160			50
Europe				9,750	10,890	11,560	12,060	11,880	11,320	11,960	12,100			24
Oceania				150	150	170	180	200	180	200	210			40
USSR				4,480	5,100	5,350	5,780	6,080	6,500	7,250	7,340			63

Source: FAO Yearbook of Fisheries Statistics 1971, Vol. 32 (Rome, 1972), Tables AO–1, AO–2. FAO Yearbook of Fisheries Statistics 1972, Vol.35 (Rome, 1973), Table AI–1.

TABLE 2. GROWTH OF OCEAN TRANSPORT: SELECTED DATA

Year	Total seaborne cargo loaded	Oil moved by sea (millions metric tons)	Dry cargo moved by sea	World tanker fleet deadweight tons (thousands)
1937	494	105	389	
1945				21,666
1950	550	225	325	
1955		350		41,623
1956		390		44,882
1957		420		50,424
1958		440		56,640
1959	990	477	513	62,657
1960		540		65,780
1961		580		68,859
1962		650		71,995
1963		710		70,179
1964		790		85,125
1965	1,677	865	812	93,171
1966	1,806	951	855	102,908
1967	1,909	1,017	892	112,366
1968	2,108	1,138	970	126,454
1969	2,308	1,271	1,037	146,029
1970	2,570	1,407	1,173	
1971	2,700	1,537	1,170	
1972	2,861	1,637	1,224	191,000
1973				201,596

Sources: UN Statistical Yearbook 1971, Table 17, p. 59, and *1972. American Petroleum Institute Petroleum Facts & Figures 1971. World Petroleum Report*, Vol. XX, 1974.

5B contains data on one source of marine-based ocean oil pollution—accidental discharge. The data are broken out by type of accident and frequency of occurrence. Finally, Table 5C presents projections made by IMCO of oil entering the oceans from marine and land-based sources to the year 2000. These data should be interpreted with considerable caution. For example, the relative and absolute decline in ocean oil pollution from land-based sources depends on the assumption that these will become subject to increasingly effective controls. Note also that the amount of gaseous emissions is very

TABLE 3. OFFSHORE OIL PRODUCTION: SELECTED DATA

A   Offshore Production of Crude Oil[a]
('000 bbl's/day)

	1960	1964	1967
Free World	396	1,272	2,356
United States	190	449	870
Latin America	25	59	77
Europe		8	10
Africa		65	165
Middle East	181	684	1,184
Far East		7	50

B   Projected Offshore Oil Production[b]

Year	Quantity (millions bbls.)	As % total world consumption (%)
1969	2.65	18
1970	2.99	19
1971	3.39	20
1972	3.82	21
1973	4.48	23
1974	5.21	25
1975	6.02	27
1976	7.16	30
1977	8.43	33
1978	9.20	35
1979	10.69	38
1980	12.04	40

[a]*Source: Offshore Petroleum Industry*, Vol. 1 (Barrows), adapted from table, p. 25.

[b]*Source:* Ibid., Vol. 1, table, p. 10.

large relative to other sources, but the amount and form reaching the oceans is unknown.[6]

While not exhaustive, the data provided in these tables do confirm that the economic value of ocean services has been and will continue to increase. External diseconomies as-

[6] See Table 7, page 84, for more detailed estimates of oil reaching the oceans.

TABLE 4. GROWTH OF OCEAN RECREATIONAL USE: SELECTED DATA

Attendance at U.S. National Seashores (rounded to nearest thousands)

	1955	1960	1965	1967	1970	1972	1973	Increase 1967–73 (%)
Assateague				738,000	1,648,000	1,698,000	2,022,000	174
Cape Cod			2,306,000	3,040,000	3,987,000	4,972,000	4,743,000	57
Cape Hatteras	264,000	467,000	1,089,000	997,400	1,227,000	1,783,000	1,711,000	72
Padre Island				195,000	721,000	883,000	937,000	380
Gulf Island							956,000	
Point Reyes				521,000	1,089,000	1,149,000	1,257,000	141

Source: U.S. Department of the Interior, National Park Service.

sociated with these activities, however, are not equivalent among activity categories, nor are they necessarily proportional to the level of the activities. To evaluate the second proposition of the thesis, that the cost of external diseconomies has been increasing, it is necessary to examine the nature and direction of the major externalities.

The case of free access and rights of capture for fisheries resources is perhaps most widely recognized and clearly documented. In a pioneering work, Gordon applied the economic theory of common property resources to fisheries and demonstrated the failure of a common property resource regime to allocate resources efficiently. In his words: "There appears, then, to be some truth in the conservative dictum that everybody's property is nobody's property. Wealth that is free for all is valued by none because he who is foolhardy enough to wait for its proper time of use will only find that it has been taken by another. . . . A factor of production that is valued at nothing in the business calculations of its users will yield nothing in income."[7] Christy and others have extended this argument and have properly emphasized the international distributional consequences of alternative arrangements to control fishing rights.

[7] H. C. Gordon, "The Economic Theory of a Common Property Resource: The Fishery," *Journal of Political Economy* (April 1954).

TABLE 5. WASTES ENTERING THE OCEANS: SELECTED DATA

A. U.S. Ocean Dumping: Types and Amounts, 1968[a]			
Waste type	Atlantic	Gulf Pacific (in '000 tons)	Total
Dredge spoils	15,808	15,300	7,320	38,428
Industrial wastes	3,013	696	981	4,690
Sewage sludge	4,477	0	0	4,477
Construction & demolition debris	574	0	0	574
Solid wastes	0	0	26	26
Explosives	15	0	0	15
Total	23,887	15,996	8,327	48,210

TABLE 5. Continued

B. Estimated Tanker Incident Pollution: Frequency and Outflow Quantity (by type of casualty) 1969 and 1970[b]

Type casualty	Quantity of outflow (metric tons)	Frequency
Breakdown	16,400	3
Collision	34,271	82
Explosion	34,046	15
Fire	4,319	19
Grounding	124,022	70
Ramming	4,657	23
Structural failure	212,367	51
Other	638	3
Total	430,720	266

C. Estimated Oil Discharges from Marine and Non-Marine Sources[c]

	1970		1980		1990		2000	
	Present LOT[d]	Min. LOT[d]	Present LOT[d]	Min. LOT[d]	Present LOT[d]	Min. LOT[d]	Present LOT[d]	Min. LOT[d]
Marine:	(millions metric tons/year)							
Tankers[e]	1.11	.48	2.83	1.25	3.85	1.66	4.52	1.92
Bulk/oil carriers	.06	.05	.16	.14	.22	.19	.25	.22
Other ships	.19	.19	.30	.30	.49	.49	.83	.83
Total (rounded)	1.3	.7	3.3	1.7	4.6	2.3	5.6	3.0
	Discharged	Reaching sea	Discharged	Reaching sea	Discharged	Reaching sea	Discharged	Reaching sea
Non-Marine[f]	30.0	1.8	22	1.8	13	1.6	10	1.3

[a]CEQ Ocean Dumping: A National Policy, Table 2.
[b]Tankers and the U.S. Energy Situation (Porricelli & Keith), Table 16.
[c]IMCO Study VI, adapted from tables IV, V.
[d]Present LOT means no change in extent or efficiency of present load on top operations; min. LOT means adoption of maximum efficiency load on top by the entire tanker fleet. See Chapter IV for discussion of LOT and alternatives.
[e]Assumes 30% tanker washings at sea.
[f]The discharged data include gaseous emissions; the reaching sea data do not, as the percent of gaseous emissions reaching the sea is unknown.

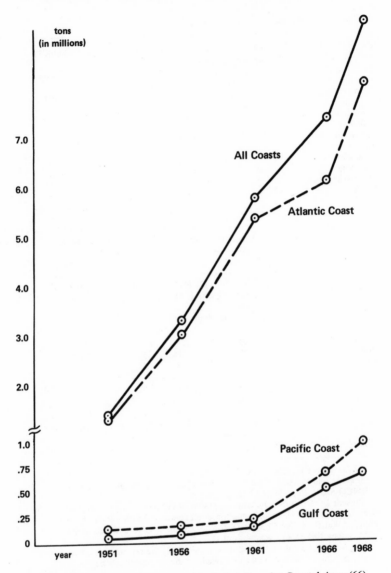

Fig. 2. Average Annual Tonnage Dumped at Sea—by Coastal Area (66).
Source: CEQ, *Ocean Dumping: A National Policy*.

The inefficiencies of free access to fisheries can be divided into two categories. First, there is the potential for physical depletion of stocks from over-fishing. Once again, without restrictions on access it is in no one's individual interest to limit fishing effort, and fishing may exceed sustainable yields of the fishing grounds. Second, even if conservation measures can be agreed upon to limit total physical catch, economic inefficiency can persist. For example, with access up to the point of maximum sustained physical yield, fishing effort can exceed the level at which the marginal or incremental productivity of fishing is equal to the marginal costs of fishing, the economically efficient solution. Each fisherman will concentrate on the average productivity of his own fishing activity, and as a result the economic rent from the fishery will be dissipated and lost by excessive fishing effort.[8] It can also be shown that free access will result in excessive fishing in relatively productive grounds and insufficient fishing in less productive grounds and that, even with national quotas, too many resources—both men and capital in the form of fishing boats—will enter the industry. In short, the economic rent of the fishery is dissipated as each fisherman pursues his own interests, decreasing the catch for others.

There is considerable evidence that both forms of external diseconomies are present and significant. Global fish catches, which had increased steadily and rapidly throughout the 1950s and 60s, held steady in 1971 and actually declined 7% in 1972. Catches from the rich grounds of the Northeast Atlantic remained constant from 1966 to 1971. Christy reports that physical depletion has occurred for a large number of stocks and is increasingly prevalent. Additionally, he states that none of the conservation measures taken has prevented the second type of inefficiency and cites studies that show an economic cost from excessive resources of $50 million in Pacific salmon and a rough estimate of $175 million for North

---

[8] More formally, the first-order condition for optimality, that the marginal costs equal marginal product will be violated as the fisherman's behavior will attempt to equalize average product and marginal cost.

Atlantic cod.[9] Certainly with regard to fisheries, the second proposition, that the cost of external diseconomies or inefficient modes of regulation have been increasing, appear valid.

Externalities associated with offshore petroleum production fall into two categories; environmental deterioration associated with incidental waste disposal, and (potential) inefficiencies in recovery because of too rapid exploitation.[10] The former will be considered in a general discussion of ocean waste disposal and environmental deterioration. The latter potential diseconomy arises from the technology of exploiting petroleum. Briefly, gas dissolved in oil in its reservoir state lowers the viscosity, specific gravity, and surface tension of the solution and provides a pressure-drive mechanism for bringing oil to the surface. The efficiency of the gas drive depends on the rate of speed of petroleum exploitation, and premature dissipation of gas reduces the quantity of petroleum that can ultimately be recovered.[11] At the same time, gas and oil fluids are fugacious and can move within an oil reservoir. If the ownership pattern of the land surface over the reservoir is privately held by several different owners, and if there are no agreements among them, then each has a strong incentive to extract oil at a rapid rate, either as a defensive move, or to capture as large as possible a share of the total recoverable oil. The consequences of unregulated production are dissipation of the natural gas drive and reduction of recoverable oil.

Without the characteristic of reduced gas drive from too rapid extraction the problem would be a straight-forward wealth distribution issue among the surface owners. With the loss of efficiency in recovery, however, petroleum exploita-

[9] See Christy. "Fisheries: Common Property, Open Access, and the Common Heritage," in *Pacem in Maribus* (Malta: Royal University of Malta Press), 2:99. The latter figure is based on data over a decade old and has undoubtedly increased.

[10] Interference with navigation may be a third diseconomy. On the other hand, it is claimed that offshore drilling rigs *improve* fishing in the area and thus generate external benefits.

[11] E. Zimmerman, *Conservation in the Production of Petroleum* (New Haven: Yale University Press, 1957).

tion again illustrates the interface between common property ownership rights and external diseconomies and suggests the importance of government intervention to increase the social welfare. Indeed, the history of legislation governing oil production within the United States can be interpreted as a process whereby local and federal government has attempted to regulate production in part in order to minimize external costs.

The same problem does not arise in the context of offshore oil production, as ownership of surface rights is not fragmented. The federal government (or, in the case of the submerged lands, those under state control) can easily require leases to be of sufficient size to prevent uneconomic exploitation. Indeed, the average size of outer continental shelf leases (as of 1969) is about 4,200 acres, compared to an average of 600 acres of continental United States government lands.[12]

The third ocean resource activity to be considered, marine transport, does not yet appear to generate pervasive and significant external costs that are internal to the activity itself, as do fisheries and unregulated oil production. Conceptually, of course, congestion of heavily traveled sea lanes should be considered an example of externalities. To the author's knowledge, however, the congestion problems that have arisen are essentially local in character and often fall within territorial waters. Accordingly, although there has been a steady and rapid increase in the economic value of ocean transport as reflected by expenditures on ocean transport, the situation of the high seas remains primarily one of excess supply, and the external costs from congestion remain small. Moreover, as is discussed presently, there has been developed a body of rules regulating maritime navigation. The 'cost' of abiding by these rules is minor and therefore they can be negotiated rather easily. Except in cases of significant conjestion, restrictions on access for transportation would be

---

[12] Data from American Petroleum Institute, *Petroleum Facts & Figures* (1971), p. 126.

economically unjustified and lead to mis-allocation of resources and inefficiency. Maritime transport does, however, generate external costs that are also external to the industry itself in the form of incidental waste disposal. These will be considered in the general discussion of ocean waste disposal.

The fourth ocean resource to be considered, mining the deep seabed for manganese nodules, is not yet in full commercial operation. Nevertheless, part of the current debate over exploitation of nodules involves an alleged externality that is internal to the activity of mining, and which again exposes the intimate link between property rights and externalities.[13] In this case however the debate centers on the correction of an external economy, or positive externality.

Briefly put, the argument is that although manganese nodules are widely distributed over the ocean floor, they vary considerably in terms of concentration per square meter, grade of ore, bottom conditions, and so forth. Considerable expenditures must be made in searching out and identifying the most easily accessible deposits. If potential investors are to underwrite these expensive exploration costs, it is argued that they must be given exclusive rights to mine large tracts—up to 8,500 square miles has been suggested. Without property rights over large areas, the initial investor with large sunk costs in exploration, can be followed by others who are given a "free ride" by the first. The initial investor must bear the full costs of exploration and development, while latecomers could simply "shadow" the first and conduct mining operations in the same area. In effect, the initial investor would be generating an economically valuable service—information resulting from exploration. An external benefit would (unwillingly) flow to the freeloaders, because the initial developer would be unable to recoup his costs by charging others for the information. In these circumstances the total amount invested in search and exploration would fall short of optimal, and resources would be inefficiently allocated.

---

[13] As in ocean transport, environmental externalities are a second result of deep sea nodule mining.

The rationale for awarding exclusive rights to nodules, or otherwise limiting access, is to internalize to the initial investor the benefits from his exploration activity. This would increase the private profitability of investment and bring it closer to the socially optimal level. Without judging the merits of the details of the argument, it is clear that it is consistent with and illustrative of the central thesis presented in this section.[14]

The fifth ocean resource service for which externalities are important is waste disposal. Wastes may be deliberately introduced into the ocean environment through ocean dumping or sewage outfalls, may arise from land-based activities and be inadvertently introduced through river runoff and atmospheric fallout, or may be the incidental result of other ocean activities—marine transport, offshore oil production, nodule mining, and so forth.

Regardless of pathway, the externalities created by waste disposal in the oceans oblige other direct and indirect users of ocean resources to bear costs. These other activities include sport and commercial fisheries (including shellfish beds), recreation, and esthetic amenities. There is also serious concern for direct human health damages as toxic pollutants, such as heavy metals, are taken up through the food chain and concentrated in fish and shellfish products. Marine transport is said to be affected, as contaminated sea water used in ships' boilers fouls intake mechanisms and harms ships' machinery. Indirect, subtle, and long-term effects on the marine ecological systems are also cited. Potentially serious costs are being passed on to future generations.

There can be little doubt that the cost of ocean environmental externalities has been increasing and that the second

[14] The second major theme of the nodule exploitation debate is the distributional question. This involves the net economic gain, or rent, from mining and how it might be distributed in accordance with the cloudy concept of the "common heritage of mankind." The nodule question neatly illustrates the dual motives of allocative efficiency and appropriation of wealth. As might be expected, the assertion of rights to sea bed resources on the part of mankind did not arise until commercial development of offshore oil and potential for nodule development were well along.

proposition of the thesis is supported. The increasing cost reflects both increases in the level of externality generating activity (e.g., oil transport) and the increasing value of resources damaged by externalities (e.g., fisheries, recreation). Both sources of increasing costs would continue in the absence of ocean environment controls.

The third proposition to be examined is that the response to increasing externality costs has been to move toward a system of user rights which forces the internalization of previously external costs and places limits on activities giving rise to these costs. There is some evidence that this process is taking place for nonenvironmental types of ocean externalities, but that the process is far from complete. With regard to fisheries resources, there are over twenty international regulatory bodies concerned with conservation of the living resources of the sea.[15] International cooperation in this area is not entirely new. The first attempt at international management of a specific stock, the protection of fur seals in the North Pacific, dates to 1911, and the first permanent regulatory fisheries body was established in 1921 by agreement between Italy and the Kingdom of the Serbs, Croats, and Slovenes to regulate Adriatic fishing. It was not until World War II, however, that the great majority of regulatory bodies were established. More importantly, the establishment of regulatory bodies does not guarantee effective control of externalities. Membership is voluntary and the measures formulated and adopted are seldom binding on the member countries. When overall catch limits are set, the criterion appears to be the level of physically sustainable yield which, as pointed out earlier, will still involve excessive fishing effort. Furthermore, the Food and Agriculture Organization (FAO) notes that a global quota does not insure a successful fishery, but rather excessive capitalization. The observations made by Christy and cited earlier confirm the conclusion that, although the problem of physical depletion of stocks (the

---

[15] For a summary account of these bodies see FAO, "Report on Regulatory Fisheries Bodies," FAO Fisheries Circular No. 138 (1972).

more obvious of fisheries externalities) has been recognized and in part acted on by the international community, the control instruments have not yet been sufficiently perfected to control the less visible economic inefficiencies involved. The final proposition, that control instruments will be increasingly chosen to minimize information costs and maximize the efficiency of the instruments themselves, has yet to occur.

A major theme in the preparations for and agenda of the Law of the Sea Conference, the right of coastal states to establish fisheries zones of up to 200 miles, can be interpreted as both an attempt to appropriate to national use part of the ocean wealth and, as a potential conservation measure, limiting the diseconomies from internationally free access and overfishing. It may be pointless to attempt to disentangle these motives. Nevertheless, it is true that by bringing fisheries within the bounds of national jurisdiction an important step in internalizing externalities is made. The costs of overfishing and stock depletion are internalized to the coastal state. This does not insure rational management, but it does present an opportunity for coastal states to take the next necessary step—limiting access by their nationals according to the principle of maximum sustainable yield or, better, preserving the maximum economic rental value of the fisheries. This is not to suggest that similar efficiencies could not be achieved with narrow fishing zones and internationally regulated access to fishing grounds. The difficulties however are more complex, for international wealth distribution would be at issue.

In a rather broad sense, the same process of internalizing externalities (mainly congestion costs) can be seen in ocean transport. The Intergovernmental Maritime Consultatiive Organization (IMCO) has been active in the promotion of maritime safety generally, including compulsory regulations for certain shipboard navigational equipment, recommendations to national governments on pilotage and port advisory services, application on a voluntary basis of ship routing and traffic separation schemes in areas of dense or converging traffic, and so forth. Major instruments concerned with safe navigation and marine safety include the 1972 revisions of the International Regulations for Preventing Collisions at Sea, the International Convention for Safety at Sea (1960 amended in 1967) and the International Convention on Load Lines (1966) in which minimum freeboards were respecified.

In general, one would expect that international agreements on such matters as ships' lanes and traffic patterns to reduce congestion costs could be fairly easily negotiated. First, the additional costs of agreeing to and abiding by such regulations is likely to be small, so that benefits would outweigh relatively minor costs for all participants. Second, preventing a collision in congested waters carries with it an incentive for each party, so that the external benefit to others of abiding by traffic regulations is accompanied by a very substantial internalized benefit.

With regard to correcting for externalities in manganese nodule exploitation, the situation is the symmetrical opposite. In the presence of external benefits, or positive externalities, free access may lead to under-utilization of the resource. This issue is at the heart of the U.S. mining interest argument and forms the basis for proposed U.S. legislation. The resolution however will be extraordinarily complicated for a number of reasons. First, of course, the nodule question is intimately tied to other Law-of-the-Sea issues and may become part of a package settlement. Second, the allocative efficiency argument is all mixed up with the wealth appropriation or rental question and, therefore, becomes an international wealth distribution issue. This has two dimensions. After nodules become commercially exploitable there will be a rental value associated with them. Now if all countries were technologically capable of nodule exploitation and there were free access, their rental value would be driven down or eliminated. In fact, the technology for exploitation is in the hands of a very few countries and, unless accompanied by international "revenue sharing" in accordance with the ambiguous common-heritage-of-mankind concept, the rental would go to the industrial countries. Moreover, the development of ocean nodules for mineral production would adversely affect the value of land-based sources who have an understandable interest in protecting the value of their deposits. Consequently, they are opposed to rapid exploitation of nodules, even if such is rational from an economic efficiency standpoint. It is not possible to explore in depth in this study these interactions between allocative efficiency and distribution.

Having reviewed the third and fourth propositions of the thesis with respect to fisheries, marine transport, and nodule exploitation, and finding that the international response to rising externality costs has been to force the internalization of externalities or to curtail externality generating activities, it remains to examine the nature of international policy toward ocean environmental externalities.

Review of Multilateral Marine Environment Policies. The outstanding characteristic of multilateral ocean environment policies is that they have evolved and are evolving in a fragmented, piecemeal fashion. The fragmentation is by type of pollutant (e.g., oil, radioactive wastes), by method of introduction to the marine environment (ocean dumping, routine tanker operation), by spatial location (territorial waters, contiguous zone, high seas) and by institutional location for policy formulation (e.g., Intergovernmental Maritime Consultative Organization [IMCO], ad hoc regional and "global" conventions, U.N. Conference on the Human Environment, Sub-Committee III of the U.N. Seabed Committee), and so forth. While policy formation is still in process, the evidence suggests that the third proposition elaborated earlier is supported as the international community moves toward restrictions on the use of the ocean environment to control and internalize externalities. A summary of these moves illustrates this.

Prior to 1972, the major multilateral ocean environment policies were as follows.[16] The Territorial Sea and Contigu-

---

[16] For more complete accounts, see M. Hardy, "International Control of Marine Pollution," *Natural Resources Journal* (April 1971); P. Swan, "International & National Approaches to Oil Pollution Responsibility: An

ous Zone Convention (1958) gives a state power to prevent pollution in territorial waters and prevent pollution in the contiguous zone, which would affect the territorial sea. At the same time there is no obligation to do so, and, furthermore, it is unclear whether action could be taken in the contiguous zone against a vessel that was not bound for territorial waters. The 1958 Convention on the Continental Shelf obliges states to protect the living resources of the sea as they undertake activities exploiting the continental shelf. There are no provisions for implementing the obligation, nor are there methods for compensating others for damages. The 1958 Geneva Convention on the High Seas obliges states to prevent marine pollution by oil (discharge or exploitation) and calls for cooperation in taking measures to prevent pollution by radioactive materials and other harmful agents. The questions of enforcement, jurisdiction, and compensation are not dealt with. Indeed, the High Seas Convention left oil pollution mainly to the 1954 International Convention for the Prevention of Pollution of the Sea by Oil (as amended in 1962 and again in 1969).

This last convention, as initially written in 1954, was directed toward the discharge of oily wastes from tanker-cleaning operations. Discharge was generally prohibited within 50 miles from land, subject to certain exemptions, and oil discharge records were required. The discharge distance was increased in the 1962 convention to 100 miles, but an earlier provision for oil-water separation devices was dropped. It is widely acknowledged that these earlier efforts at controlling routine oil discharges were relative failures. The reasons are straightforward. The detection of oil spills and assignment of responsibility to specific vessels is difficult. Shore facilities for receiving oily wastes have been inadequate and have encouraged ocean discharge. Enforcement has been left to flag states, who have little incentive for vigorous action. The convention was not universally ratified.

Emerging Regime for a Global Problem," *Oregon Law Review* 50 (Spring 1971); and W. Ross, *Oil Pollution as an International Problem* (University of Victoria, 1973).

In 1969 there was further activity with respect to marine oil pollution, with the focus shifting toward accidental discharge and toward remedial rather than preventive measures. The International Convention relating to Intervention on the High Seas in Cases of Oil Pollution Casualties (Public Law Convention) permits a coastal state to take measures on the high seas to protect its coast from pollution following a maritime casualty. The convention is a curious mixture of boldness and caution. It explicitly states that intervention rights do not affect the principle of freedom of the high seas, it exempts warships and government vessels in non-commercial operation, it only applies to pollution from oil, and then only in the case of a maritime casualty. In all events, the intervention measures (including the ultimate measure of destroying the vessel and cargo) must be proportionate to the actual or threatened damage, and if the measures are disproportionate, compensation must be given to the injured parties. Despite these restrictive provisions, the convention should be considered an innovation in the development of controls over pollution-generating activities. It explicitly permits defensive action on the part of a potential victim in international waters. It is not limited to oil tankers, but includes oil pollution damages from other vessels. Finally, intervention for protection of coastal states' interests is not limited to potential damage to state-owned properties, but is extended to include living marine resources and the livelihood of citizens engaged in fishing, tourism, and so forth. On balance it should be considered a small but significant landmark in the ongoing process of restricting pollution-generating activities.

The 1969 International Convention on Civil Liability for Oil Pollution Damage is limited to seagoing vessels carrying oil as cargo. The convention attempts to unify international rules for establishing liability and setting compensation. Compensation is set at $135 for each ton of the ship's tonnage, not to exceed $14 million dollars for each incident.[17] Liability is exempted in several situations, including acts of war and

[17] Unlimited liability if the accident is the result of actual fault on the part of the owner.

natural phenomenon of exceptional, inevitable and irrestible character ("Acts of God").

Shortcomings of the 1969 Civil Liability Convention were recognized, and the 1971 International Convention on the Establishment of an International Fund for Compensation for Oil Pollution Damages was an attempt to correct them. The Fund Convention increased the limits of compensation to $36 million per incident (with a possibility for increasing this to $72 million). Acts of God no longer exempt the shipowner from liability. To lighten the burden on shipowners, the fund will indemnify them for payments in excess of certain minimums, thus shifting some of the financial burden on to oil importers. A fund is established, with payments by oil importers in proportion to tonnage imported.

Despite these improvements, the Fund Convention remains incomplete. Specifically, it is remedial and not preventive. It applies only to damages done within territorial waters, it applies only to accidents and not routine discharge, and its liability limits are far short of the potential financial cost of a major near-shore oil spill. Perhaps most important, neither the Liability Convention, nor the Fund Convention has been ratified by the United States. The Intervention Convention has been ratified by the United States but has not yet come into force, pending ratification by three additional states.

The U.N. Conference on the Human Environment (the Stockholm Conference) has also been a motivating force in formulating ocean environment policy. Its influence has been both of a specific nature, resulting somewhat indirectly in the 1972 London Convention on the Prevention of Marine Pollution by Dumping of Wastes and Other Matters ("Ocean Dumping Convention"), and of a more general nature in stating principles and recommendations governing the environmental use of marine resources.[18]

[18] For a general discussion of ocean dumping, see C. Pearson, "Control of Ocean Dumping," *SAIS Review* 17, no. 1 (Fall 1972). Peter Thacher has evaluated the Stockholm Conference activities regarding marine pollution. See Thacher, "Assessment and Control of Marine Pollution: The Stockholm Conference and Their Efficacy," *Stanford Journal of International Studies* 7 (Spring 1973).

It is difficult to assess the actual results of Stockholm. In part this is because the process of conference preparation and participation can be viewed as an objective that was more important than the Declaration of Principles and Recommendations contained in the Action Plan itself. There is much validity to this view; preparations for the conference did indeed force governments and individuals into awareness of international environmental issues. For example, in the area of marine pollution, an Intergovernmental Working Group on Marine Pollution (IWG) was established to survey the entire range of the problem, regardless of source, and to formulate recommendations to the conference. The IWG worked with GESAMP (Group of Experts on the Scientific Aspects of Marine Pollution), reviewing marine pollutants according to their hazards and preparing an initial draft treaty on ocean dumping.

The Declaration of Principles of the Stockholm Conference, while not binding in international law, clearly lays down the obligations of states regarding the marine environment. Principle 7 states that "States shall take all possible steps to prevent pollution of the seas by substances that are liable to create hazards to human health, to harm living resources and marine life, to damage amenities, or interfere with other legitimate uses of the sea." Principle 21 declares: "States have, in accordance with the Charter of the United Nations and the principles of international law, the sovereign right to exploit their own resources pursuant to their own environmental policies, and the responsibility to ensure that activities within their jurisdiction or control do not cause damage to the environment of other States or of areas beyond the limits of national jurisdiction."

Principle 21 is especially noteworthy as it captures in one sentence a fundamental ambivalence present at the conference. States remained attached to the concept of sovereign rights within their territory, but acknowledged that they share a unified environment. Despite the nod given to exploiting one's own resources, the principle is an injunction against damaging the environment of another state and, furthermore, against damaging any area beyond its national jurisdiction. This is a significant development, for it advances the states' obligations beyond transnational pollution to protecting an international common property resource, the high seas. Moreover, the oceans are to be protected from both land-based activities and, presumably through the phrase "within their jurisdiction or control," from marine-based activities. For example, flag states will be responsible for pollution caused by ships sailing under their flag. While these declarations of principle require implementing measures, they do exert some pressure and over the longer run contribute to the process of limiting rights on the high seas and curtailing activities causing environmental externalities.

Within the Recommendations for Action, the delegates cautiously recognized that controlling marine-based pollution sources would leave untouched major land-based sources, and in Recommendation 92 recommended that "governments take early action to adopt effective national measures for the control of all significant sources of marine pollution including land-based sources, and concert and coordinate their actions regionally and where appropriate on a wider international basis."

In addition the conference recommended that governments "accept and implement available instruments on the control of the marine sources of marine pollution" (meaning the 1954 Convention on the Pollution of the Sea by Oil, as amended, as well as the IAEA Registry of Radioactive Waste Discharges and IMCO codes regarding dangerous goods, ship construction, traffic lanes, etc.), and that governments ensure that "the provisions of these instruments are complied with by ships flying their flags *and by ships operating in areas under their jurisdiction* (emphasis added)."[19]

---

[19] The United States had reservations concerning this last recommendation, presumably fearing that coastal state exercise of environmental rights might limit navigational freedoms. It opposed the whole of Recommendation 92, stating that, while it agreed with much of the underlying principle, the proper forum for consideration would be the 1973 IMCO Conference and the forthcoming Law of the Sea Conference.

The ocean dumping convention that had been worked on in London (1971) and Reykjavik (April 1972) was not completed by conference time. In lieu of agreement, the delegates recommended convening a special conference in London later in the year to finish work on the convention. The resulting document, the Convention on the Prevention of Marine Pollution by Dumping of Wastes and other Matter, was agreed to in November 1972. The content of the Ocean Dumping Convention will be analyzed presently; here we simply note that it represents yet another partial attempt to control marine pollution, and that it parallels in certain important respects U.S. domestic legislation on ocean dumping (1972) and a regional ocean dumping convention for the North Sea concluded in 1972.

The last, and most recent global multilateral effort at controlling marine pollution was the 1973 International Convention for the Prevention of Pollution from Ships.[20] Again, this convention will be analyzed in some detail below; here we note that the objective of the convention was to correct the shortcomings of previous instruments, not only for oil pollution but for the transport of other noxious substances. In short, it represents a comprehensive effort to regulate discharge from ships and bring this particular source of marine pollution within tighter limits.

Not all of these conventions are in force; not all have effective means for implementation. Nevertheless, this review does support the third proposition of the expanded Demsetz thesis—the international response to increasing environmental externality costs has been to develop systems of user rights that either force the internalization of previously external costs, or limit the activities giving rise to these costs. The process of marine environment policy formation can be seen, then, as similar to that under way for other ocean resource uses, including fisheries, marine transport, and manganese nodules.

[20] The work accomplished by Subcommittee III of the U.N. Seabed Committee in preparation for the Law of the Sea Conference is discussed on page 56, below.

FURTHER CONSIDERATIONS IN INTERPRETING
OCEAN ENVIRONMENT CONTROLS

Negotiating Environmental Controls

The controls reviewed earlier all share the characteristic that they are essentially voluntary agreements among sovereign states. This voluntary characteristic is evident in the decision to participate in the policy formation process, effects the content of the agreements, and again is evident in the speed or lack thereof in the implementation of the controls. The voluntary character of the agreements also distinguishes multilateral control measures for international environmental resources from domestic controls over domestic resources. The process of formulating domestic policy, while far from perfect, has the very considerable advantages of ultimately being capable of requiring compliance and having instruments for redressing inequities resulting from forced compliance.

In principle, voluntary agreements among states will not lead to optimal levels of environmental quality for the oceans unless there are good mechanisms in place for international compensation, or unless states adopt a global rather than a national welfare perspective. Neither of these can be relied upon with certainty.

Consider the following. Prior to any multilateral agreements concerning the environmental use of the oceans, it will be in each state's interest to pursue ocean pollution abatement up to the point at which the marginal cost of abatement to itself is just equal to the marginal benefit *to itself* from avoiding ocean pollution damages. However, some part of the benefit from abatement will accrue to other states (that is, abatement by one country will prevent damages to other countries). The first country will not, however, include these benefits in its calculus, and it will be rational from the individual country perspective to limit abatement effects to levels below the global optimum.[21] As all countries act on

---

[21] The argument could be couched in terms of external costs. Pollution-generating activities will be expanded beyond their global optimum as

their individual welfare, the situation will be one of reciprocal mutual externalities.

If a perfect private market among states existed, in which the external benefits from pollution abatement could be "purchased," and if there were accurate knowledge of the value of the benefits, then negotiations among states might be relied upon to achieve a more optimal use of ocean environmental resources. A state conferring external benefits from additional abatement activities could be compensated by other states (or, to use the more common terms, a network of bribes from victims to polluters would develop). Alternatively, if implicit rights to ocean resource users were given to beneficial users rather than polluters, and there were a perfect market among states, a network of compensation payments for damages done by environmental degradation would develop. If polluters could not afford the charges set by victims, this would constitute prima facie evidence that the opportunity cost of ocean pollution abatement—by treatment, design modification, or alternative disposal methods—was less than the potential damage of ocean pollution. Although no bargain would be struck and no compensation payment made, resources would still be allocated correctly.

Whether one views the process as a network of bribes from victims to polluters or a network of compensation from polluters to victims, there is every reason to believe that some international transfers would have to be made. Even if one assumes that all parties are beneficial users of the oceans (transport, fisheries, tourism, etc.) and all parties generate external costs on others, the net position of individual countries will not be zero, either in terms of their external costs absorbed net of external costs imposed on others, or in terms of the benefits received from abatement by others net of benefits conferred on others by their own abatement activities. That is, by moving from a preagreement position to a

---

individual countries fail to take external costs imposed on others into account.

globally more optimal position, through either compensation or bribes, there will be an increase in global welfare and a change in the relative welfare of states. The change in relative welfare will come about if there are transfers among countries.

In general, if the "perfect" market exists, and if a system of compensation is assumed, the relative welfare of those countries that are characterized by high beneficial use of ocean resources and low abatement costs will improve, and the relative welfare of those countries which are characterized by low beneficial use of the oceans and high abatement costs will deteriorate. The reverse will be true if a system of bribes from victims to polluters is in place. Starting from a situation of unimpeded pollution, a system of bribes would, however, make victims relatively worse off, but would in general improve their absolute welfare.

More realistically, an international market for external costs or external benefits from abatement does not exist, and negotiations among states are often constrained to solutions that do not call for international transfers. There is still scope, however, for improving the preagreement position in which each country pursued abatement up to the point at which its marginal abatement costs equaled the marginal benefit it received from damages avoided. The operative constraint in this situation would be an agreement in which each state is made no worse off than before. Each state considering an agreement would calculate the net benefit to itself of the agreement and, if non-negative, would presumably agree. In turn, the net benefit would be a comparison of its preagreement position—external costs incurred less external costs imposed on others—with its post-agreement position. If the benefits from abatement by others equaled or exceeded its own abatement costs, the move would be justified.

A numerical example will help clarify this fundamental point in international negotiations for the reduction of environmental diseconomies. Consider the following table, which is a hypothetical matrix of damage flows from externalities, the abatement costs of alternative corrective measures, and the net gains or losses from various abatement measures. For simplicity we assume two countries, Country A and the rest of the world denoted Country B. Column 1 shows the damage flow from A to itself from its own ocean pollution activities, and the costs to A of abating its own pollution. Column 2 shows the damage from B to A as the result of B's activities. Column 3 shows total damages received by A from all sources, the cost to itself for its own abatement, and its net gain or loss from alternative abatement activities. It is the horizontal sum of columns 1 and 2. Columns 4, 5, and 6 do the same for Country B; 4 is the damage flow from B to itself as the result of its own pollution activities, column 5 is the flow of damages from A to B, and column 6 shows total damages received by B from all sources, the cost to itself of its own abatement, and its net gain or loss from alternative abatement activities. Finally, column 7 is the sum of columns 3 and 6 and shows global welfare.

Rows 1 through 6 show the possibilities for unilateral action by either A or B; rows 7 through 12 show how global and national welfare can increase by international agreement when unilateral action would not be undertaken; rows 13 through 18 show how international agreement may fail to achieve global welfare gains if there is not an adequate international compensation mechanism in place.

Consider first row 1, which shows damage flows before any environmental controls, unilateral or international. Country A generates total external damages of $12M, of which it absorbs $4M itself and passes off $8M to B. In turn, B generates damages of $8M, of which it absorbs $5M and passes $3M back to A. Global damages are then $20M, of which A absorbs $7M and B absorbs $13M. Assume a pollution abatement measure, say Load on Top, for oil pollution, with real costs reflected in higher transport costs. Row 2 shows the additional transport cost to A to be $2M, and $3M to B from LOT. Assume also that LOT reduces pollution damages but does not eliminate them, so that the residual damages after LOT are described in row 3.

TABLE 6. FLOWS OF DAMAGES, ABATEMENT COST, WELFARE CHANGES, BY COUNTRY AND GLOBALLY

	Flow to A from action by A	Flow to A from action by B	Total flow to A (Col. 1 + Col. 2)	Flow to B from action by B	Flow to B from action by A	Total flow to B (Col. 4 + Col. 5)	Net global flow (Col. 3 + Col. 6)
	(1)	(2)	(3)	(4)	(5)	(6)	(7)
1) Damage flow prior to EC	4.0	3.0	7.0	5.0	8.0	13.0	20.0
2) Abatement cost of LOT	2.0		2.0	3.0		3.0	5.0
3) Residual damage after LOT by A & B	1.0	.5	1.5	1.0	4.0	5.0	6.5
4) Welfare gain: unilateral LOT by A	1.0		1.0		4.0	4.0	5.0
5) Welfare gain: unilateral LOT by B		2.5	2.5	1.0		1.0	3.5
6) Welfare gain: unilateral LOT A & B	1.0	2.5	3.5	1.0	4.0	5.0	8.5
7) Residual damage after LOT by A & B	1.0	.5	1.5	1.0	4.0	5.0	6.5
8) Abatement costs of segregated ballasting	.8		.8	.5		.5	1.3
9) Residual damage after segregated ballasting by A & B	.25	.25	.5	.5	2.0	2.5	3.0

10) Welfare gain: unilateral segregated ballasting by A	-.05				2.0	2.0	1.95
11) Welfare gain: unilateral segregated ballasting by B		.25	.25	0		0	.25
12) Welfare gain agreement on segregated ballasting by A & B	-.05	.25	.2	0	2.0	2.0	2.2
13) Residual damage after LOT by A & B	1.0	.5	1.5	1.0	4.0	5.0	6.5
14) Abatement costs of segregated ballasting + double bottoms	2.0			1.2		1.2	3.2
15) Residual damages after segregated ballasting & double bottoms by A & B	2.0		2.0	0	0	0	0
16) Welfare gain: unilateral action by A	-1.0		0		4.0	4.0	3.0
17) Welfare gain: unilateral action by B		.5	.5	-.2		-.2	.3
18) Welfare gain: agreement between A & B	-1.0	.5	-.5	-.2	4	3.8	3.3

Now, even without international agreement it is in the interest of County A to institute LOT. Row 4 shows that the net welfare gain to A from unilateral LOT is $1M—the reduction in damages to itself by itself, less the abatement cost, is positive (4 minus 2 minus 1 equals 1). At the same time, it confers a benefit (reduction in damage) of $4M on Country B, so that the global welfare gain is 5. Country A should be willing to undertake this action on a unilateral basis. The same holds for Country B, as shown in row 5; if it unilaterally undertakes LOT it reduces damages to itself by $4M at an abatement cost of $3M, for a net gain in welfare of $1M. It also confers a benefit (reduction in damage) to A of $2.5M, so that the global welfare gain is $3.5M. We could expect individual states acting in their own self-interest and without any international agreement to simultaneously undertake this abatement measure, with a net global welfare gain of $8.5M, of which $3.5M accrues to Country A and $4.5M accrues to Country B, as described in line 6.

Notice, however, that there are residual damages after LOT, as described in row 3 and repeated in row 7, and that further welfare gains may be possible. Row 8 assumes a further abatement measure that we call segregated ballasting. The assumed costs of instituting segregated ballasting for A and B are given in row 8, and the assumed residual damages after instituting segregated ballasting are described in row 9. In this case, however, we cannot rely on unilateral action to secure additional gains. Row 10 shows that unilateral action by Country A would reduce the damage it does to itself by 0.75M, from $1M to $0.25M, but abatement cost would be $0.8M and would exceed the benefits to itself. It would have no reason to include the incidental benefit to B of $2M in its own calculations and, despite the improvement in global welfare of $1.95M, the action would not be justified by national welfare criteria. Row 11 shows a somewhat similar situation for Country B—the abatement costs from unilateral action by B would equal the damage reduction, and it would be indifferent to the measure, despite a global welfare gain of $0.25M.

With unilateral action ruled out, international agreement between A and B, committing each to segregated ballasting, becomes feasible. Row 12 demonstrates that agreed joint action by both would improve the global welfare ($2.2M) and would leave each party in a better position ($0.2M to A, $2.0M to B). If strict equality in gains were not a constraint, we would expect voluntary negotiations to arrive at this solution.

Finally, to complete the numerical example, we note that even with LOT and segregated ballasting some residual damages would remain. Assume a third pollution abatement measure, segregated ballasting coupled with double bottoms. Row 13 repeats the residual damages (after LOT) shown in lines 3 and 7. The assumed costs of segregated ballasting plus double bottoms are shown in row 14, and residual damages, assumed zero, are shown in row 15.[22] Row 16 shows that from a national welfare perspective unilateral action by A would not be justified; row 17 shows the same for unilateral action by B, despite the improvement in global welfare associated with each. Nor can we be certain that an international agreement will succeed. Row 18 demonstrates that an international agreement between A and B would be globally rational and, indeed, lead to a greater net welfare gain than segregated ballasting alone ($3.3M vs. $2.2M). But the welfare position of Country A would show an absolute decline of $0.5M, and unless it could be compensated by an amount not less than $0.5M it would, presumably, not enter the agreement. Consequently, to attain the global optimum position some international compensation from B to A would have to be forthcoming.

Several general conclusions emerge. First, the more nearly the costs of ocean pollution are fully borne by the polluting country the less serious is the international negotiation problem. External costs are internalized to a country when polluted river runoff damages its own shellfish beds. While

---

[22] The data are illustrative—in practice we would not expect to proceed with abatement to the point of zero residual damages.

there is no guarantee of optimal policy response by the national government, the matrix in which environmental control policy is formulated is considerably less complex. Second, multilateral negotiations can improve the allocation of environmental resources, but unless there are mechanisms for deliberate welfare transfers among countries, either in the form of bribes or compensation, it is unlikely that ocean environmental quality will be adequately protected. In this connection it is interesting to observe that the movement in international law regarding ocean environment is from de facto rights awarded to polluters, toward an increasingly strong regime of rights to beneficial users. Thus, as a practical matter the relative welfare of beneficial users is increasing, and if there were a "market" we would expect to see compensation flows rather than bribery networks. Third, it can be asserted that the less disparity there is among countries as to their net welfare change resulting from multilateral abatement measures, the closer will be an international agreement without compensation to the optimal. At the limit, if all countries had identical beneficial interests and identical ocean pollution abatement costs, no compensation would be required, and voluntary agreements would be an efficient method for protecting the marine environment.[23]

Environmental Controls within Law-of-the-Sea Framework

The discussion thus far in this section has implicitly assumed that marine environmental controls are formulated in isolation from other law-of-the-sea issues. This is partially

[23] Something of the same situation prevails in economic integration among developing countries. While integration may benefit the region as a whole, the minimum constraint on negotiating the agreement is that each member is made no worse off. As members can expect to differ as to their net benefit position as a result of membership, reasonable reciprocity in the distribution of benefits is a necessary condition for rapid integration. In turn, reciprocity of benefits will not result automatically from the integration process, and formal methods must be sought to redistribute the integration benefits. These may be direct transfers of income, regional allocation of new investments, or others. In the context of tariff negotiations, global welfare can be increased, but the distribution of welfare domestically will be altered. Governments have attempted to compensate the disadvantaged groups through internal

correct. The major forum has been the Intergovernmental Maritime Consultative Organization (IMCO), and IMCO's mandate does not extend to major ocean policy issues, such as the width of the territorial sea, disputes over fishing rights, passage through international straits, and so forth. More realistically, however, ocean environment controls both condition and are conditioned by these major ocean issues. The environmental fate of the oceans will be decided in conjunction with the resolution of these other issues, and most probably as the incidental result of domestic environmental activities.

The 1973 London Conference on the Prevention of Pollution by Ships presents a vivid illustration of the intrusion of other ocean issues in forming marine environment policy. Two questions that lie at the core of most ocean issues were raised and nearly succeeded in sinking the conference. Both concerned jurisdiction—the areal extent of national jurisdiction over ocean space, and the rights of coastal states to establish more stringent environmental measures for the protection of their environment within areas under their jurisdiction.

With regard to the areal extent of jurisdiction, which directly involves most important law-of-the-sea issues, the question at London was the extent to which a country could extend its environmental jurisdictional zone. Ultimately, the question was side-stepped. The convention obliges a country to prohibit and punish violations "within its jurisdiction, or to refer them to the flag state for prosecution." It intentionally avoided any resolution of the areal jurisdictional question and, in line with the U.S. position, deferred the matter to the forthcoming Law of the Sea Conference. Thus there was no endorsement or condemnation of the asymmetrical situation in which Canada claims a 100 mile environmental zone and the United States 12 miles.

---

redistribution, using trade adjustment assistance type measures. The international compensation is made through product prices themselves and, therefore, does not pose a barrier to optimal agreements.

The conference also avoided a resolution of the rights of coastal states to establish more stringent measures within their ocean jurisdiction. Presumably, these measures would include rigorous ship discharge standards and specifications regarding ship design and pollution control equipment. The United States, as a major maritime power with a strong interest in unimpeded commercial navigation, wishes to see internationally uniform environmental controls over marine transit, rather than a patchwork of differing coastal state standards. Article 8 of the draft convention, prepared prior to the conference, explicitly permitted states to establish more stringent standards under certain conditions. This article became the most controversial element at the conference and, following considerable pressure by the United States, was omitted from the final document, the question being deferred to the Law of the Sea Conference.[24]

That environmental policy issues are naturally tied to other ocean policy issues and cannot be fully separated is quite clear. The point to be made here, however, goes further. Environmental policy issues are being consciously linked to other law-of-the-sea (LOS) issues in the negotiations themselves. For example, an analysis of the lessons of the London Conference for the Law of the Sea negotiations drew the conclusion that the United States would lose the pollution jurisdiction question embodied in Article 8 in the forthcoming Law of the Sea Conference if it is considered in isolation from other major LOS issues.

The interesting question is whether a strategy of linkages will improve or harm the chances for a rational marine environment policy. An argument can be made on either side. Conceptually, the inclusion of several rather than a single

[24] As described by Russell Train, Chairman of the U.S. Delegation, ''This really was the most difficult element in the Conference because it involved such divergent points of view *not really of an environmental nature*, or even a maritime nature, but of national interest generally.'' *Hearings on the 1973 IMCO Conference* p. 9 (emphasis is added). At the same time the United States itself is considering imposition of higher standards on U.S. vessels engaged in coastwise trade out of Alaskan ports.

issue in negotiations sharply increases the number of feasible agreements, and offers the participants a broader range of alternatives. The "units of currency" for trade-offs, bargains, side deals, and the like are augmented, and these can be used to effect the compensation that was earlier argued to be desirable. That is, by increasing the number of issues are to be simultaneously determined, a player in the negotiations can offer a concession in one field of interest and take payment in quite a different area. In a broad sense, the international transfer mechanism is improved and the prospects for an agreement in which all participants are benefited improves.[25]

Unfortunately, it is not at all clear that a linked negotiating process will improve the environmental portion of the ultimate agreement. Particularly, if states perceive their environmental interests to be small relative to others, such as unimpeded maritime commerce, naval mobility, rights to offshore oil and gas, and so on, the environmental interest may, on balance, be sacrificed to attain other objectives in the negotiations. This is even more troubling if environmental interest groups are weak domestically in comparison to other interest groups affecting the national position in the negotiations.[26]

There is a conflict of opinion as to whether broad environmental zones would increase or decrease effective protection of the environment. For example, Hargrove argues that a broad zone under coastal state control would preclude the international community from placing any effective restraints on environmental harm done on a national level, as it is now precluded from controlling degradation within national territories. The result would be a major seaward extension of resource exploitation and accompanying environmental deterioration. In contrast, Canada has argued strongly that

---

[25] Something of the same logic supports multilateral as opposed to bilateral trade negotiations.

[26] Shinn is also concerned that the ocean environment can easily be sacrificed to other interests. See R. Shinn, *The International Politics of Marine Pollution Control* (New York: Praeger, 1974).

coastal states, by virtue of their special interests in maintaining the quality of their coastal waters, should be accorded broad environmental zones to accomplish this protection. In essence, the argument turns on whether coastal states are capable of perceiving and acting in their true interest in preserving the marine environment.[27]

There are other reasons for caution in evaluating the role of international negotiations on marine pollution. First, the information feed-back system for international common property resources, such as the oceans, is less reliable and has a longer time lag than does direct transnational pollution. If state A degrades a common river and harms state B downstream, it is relatively easy to detect the damage and identify the state responsible. In contrast, ocean deterioration may be long-term, subtle, and indirect, so that the perception of damage lags considerably the fact of damage. Because the pathways of pollutants are poorly known, it may be impossible to identify major source countries. Without knowledge of damages and resources, international negotiations for marine pollution control operate under severe handicaps.[28]

Second, there does not seem to be any good prospect for international control of the major source of marine pollution—river runoffs and land-based atmospheric pollution that finds its way into ocean space. The combination of the Ocean Dumping and Prevention of Pollution From Ships Conventions will strengthen controls over marine-based pollution sources if and when ratified by the signatory states.[29] At the same time it is not apparent how these two conven-

---

[27] L. Hargrove, *Testimony at the Hearings on S.1067, S.1070, S.1351. Before the Subcommittee on Oceans & Atmosphere of the Senate Committee on Commerce*, 93rd Cong., 1st Sess., Serial No. 93–46, p. 130 (1973).

[28] In addition, international law regarding direct transnational pollution is more highly developed than is the law regarding pollution of international common property resources.

[29] The danger of accidental discharge from supertankers remains and is graphically described by Noël Mostert in a series of *New Yorker* articles (May 1974). Porricelli and Keith, however, support supertankers on safety grounds in an exceptionally interesting study. J. Porricelli and V. Keith, "Tankers and the U.S. Energy Situation—an Economic & Environmental Analysis," paper presented at the Philadelphia Section of the Society of Naval Architects and Marine Engineers, Dec. 7, 1973.

tions "constitute an effective effort to carry out a comprehensive strategy to control the pollution of the seas"[30] unless they are accompanied by major *domestic* environmental control efforts.

While the Declaration of Principles in the Stockholm documents obliges states to avoid environmental harm to areas beyond national jurisdiction, it remains ineffective without implementing measures. Even a modest recommendation by Canada at Stockholm, which would have set up a world registry of polluted river discharges into the oceans, was not acceptable as it was seen to be in conflict with national sovereignty.

In preparation for the LOS Conference the question of land-based sources of marine pollution has generally been avoided as beyond the scope of the conference and, for practical purposes, not a matter for international action. An exception to this was a 1971 proposal by Malta, which inter alia would give an ocean authority certain powers for controlling land-based pollution sources, but this approach was dropped early on. Even such a strong supporter of marine pollution control as Canada concluded that "Where marine pollution is brought about by substances entering the sea via the atmosphere or continental runoff as a result of land-based activities, this problem might best be dealt with through a combination of national action and international cooperation in other (non-LOS) forums."

There is no prospect that the Law of the Sea Conference will reach back to effectively curtail land-based sources of marine pollution—the exercise of national sovereignty will insure this. Consequently, the environmental destiny of the oceans will rest in large measure on the vigor with which individual countries pursue environmental quality goals domestically and will not be subject to international negotiations.[31]

---

[30] Russell Train, *Testimony at Hearings on the 1973 IMCO Conference on Marine Pollution from Ships.*

[31] This may be too pessimistic. See, for example, the 1974 Paris Convention negotiated by fourteen West European states concerning marine pollution from land-based sources.

The Functional Breakup of Ocean Space

This chapter started by postulating that increasing externality costs associated with the historic legal regime of the oceans, freedom of the seas, and free access to the resources therein, has been a motivating force for a new regime that would increasingly internalize externalities. It was shown that this process, although obscured at points and far from complete, can be seen in fisheries, marine transport, nodule exploitation, and environmental control. The process is greatly assisted by the functional breakup of ocean space.

What is happening is the assertion of rights by states over ocean space by function, or the extension of jurisdiction for limited purposes. The motive is both wealth appropriation and internalization of externalities. The United States started the process with the 1948 Truman Proclamation, asserting rights over the resources of the continental shelf and, in particular, petroleum reserves. Sanctioned by the 1958 Convention on the Continental Shelf, the Truman Proclamation effectively distinguishes between the right to exploit continental seabed resources by coastal states and the rights of fishing, navigation, etc. open to all nations on the traditional freedom of the seas, free access basis. The next major move was the assertion of rights to fisheries resources within zones of up to 200 miles, particularly on the part of West Coast Latin American countries. Again ocean space was being broken down according to function. More recently Canada unilaterally declared an environmental zone of 100 miles into the Arctic. The action followed the path-breaking (literally) voyage of the Manhattan through Arctic waters, exploring the prospects for delivering Alaskan crude. In this case Canada asserted rights to control marine transit and hence minimize pollution danger to the fragile Northern environment. Similarly, the 1970 U.S. Draft Treaty on Law of the Sea issues split ocean space three ways—territorial waters in which the coastal state was fully sovereign, an intermediate zone in which coastal states had special but limited rights, and the high seas.

The U.S. position recognized the pressures for, and contributed to, the functional breakup of ocean space. It proposed the extension of territorial seas to 12 miles (accompanied by agreement on free transit through and over international straits). Beyond the 12-mile limit or a 200 meter isobath, and with respect to seabed resources, the United States proposed an intermediate zone in which coastal states and the international community would share rights. The coastal state would regulate exploration and exploitation of mineral resources but be subject to international pollution standards and obliged to share with the international community some of the revenues from exploitation. Again the thrust was to divide ocean space by function.

From the point of view of the Law-of-the-Sea negotiations, the unbundling of rights to ocean space is a positive move. The justification for the old regime of freedom of the high seas was being eroded by increasing externality costs and by the desire to appropriate to national use the new wealth of the oceans. At the same time, the various uses of ocean space do not demand the same degree of national control. Maritime commerce and military security are seen to be best served by preserving the traditional regime; fisheries need either effective national or international control, as does the protection of the marine environment. Offshore petroleum is too tempting a prize to imagine that anything but coastal state control would follow.

The unbundling of rights to ocean resources permits a selective arrangement in which rights to certain resources, such as maritime transit, can be guaranteed, while other rights accrue to coastal states (perhaps under some international supervision). All this frees up the negotiation process and, just as the linkage of issues increases the currency of negotiations, the functional breakup of ocean space and unbundling of rights to its resources increases the scope for trade-offs, bargains, and, ultimately, the possibilities for an agreement itself.

III. ANALYSIS OF THE OCEAN DUMPING CONVENTION

The two major accomplishments in multilateral control over marine-based ocean pollution are the 1972 Convention on the Prevention of Marine Pollution by Dumping of Wastes and Other Matter (Ocean Dumping Convention) and the 1973 International Convention for the Prevention of Pollution from Ships.[1] In this chapter we briefly describe the provisions of the first convention and analyze its content from an economic perspective. The purpose is to bring the earlier conceptual discussion closer to reality, and to determine the extent to which economic considerations have contributed to the formation of these two multilateral ocean environment measures.

The two conventions are somewhat dissimilar for analytical purposes. The Ocean Dumping Convention requires member countries to act individually in carrying out the obligations of the convention. Accordingly, it requires domestic regulatory bodies to implement and enforce the provisions of the convention. With the exception of materials listed in Annex I of the convention—for which ocean dumping is prohibited—the convention does not set forth specific obligations that can be analyzed by using traditional benefit-cost techniques. Consequently, economic analysis that goes beyond a discussion of the general rationality of the provisions and their intent requires an examination of the domestic implementing regulations and, more importantly, the actual practices followed by countries as they carry out their obligations.

In contrast, the Convention on the Prevention of Pollution from Ships lays down some rather specific obligations regard-

---

[1] In addition these are important regional agreements. See the North Sea Ocean Dumping Convention (1972) and the 1974 Paris Convention on marine pollution from land-based sources, previously noted, and a Baltic Sea Convention done in 1974 by seven Baltic riparian states.

ing ship construction, design, and operating performance which, conceptually, can be evaluated within a benefit-cost framework. Thus, for analytical purposes, the convention itself and not domestic implementation and enforcement is the object of inquiry.[2]

OCEAN DUMPING CONVENTION PROVISIONS AND RELATED LEGISLATION

Ocean dumping is the deliberate disposal at sea by ship, barge, and dredge of liquid and solid wastes, including the deliberate disposal of unserviceable and obsolete vessels themselves. Dumped materials include dredge spoils, industrial wastes, sewage sludge, garbage, explosives and munitions, and demolition debris. Evidence suggests that ocean dumping has been increasing due to increasing wastes per capita, exhaustion of low-cost urban sites for landfill operations, more stringent environmental standards for onshore air and water waste disposal, and other factors.

The convention requires states to take all practical steps to prevent dumping that would create hazards to human health, harm marine life, or damage amenities. To this end, it requires regulation of dumping by national governments according to the nature of the dumped material. Three classes of material are set forth—Annex I substances for which dumping is prohibited, the so-called blacklist; Annex II substances for which special permits must be granted, the 'grey' list; and all other materials for which a prior general permit is required. Included on the black list are organohalogen compounds (DDT, PBC, etc.), mercury and cadmium, persistent plastics, oil taken on board for the purpose of dumping, high level radioactive wastes, and biological and chemical warfare agents.[3]

---

[2] See Appendix I for the text of the Ocean Dumping Convention and for a comparison of the main features of the Convention on the Prevention of Pollution from Ships with the earlier Convention on the Prevention of Pollution by Oil (1954, as amended) which it supersedes.

[3] Not to include trace contaminants of the first four. Note that high level radioactive wastes have not been internationally defined.

Annex II contains the grey list, for which special permits must be issued. The substances included are arsenic, lead, copper, zinc, organosilicon compounds, cyanides, fluorides, certain pesticides; acids, alkalis containing beryllium, chromium, nickel, and vanadium; containers, scrap metal, and bulky wastes that may interfere with fishing and navigation; and radioactive wastes not found in Annex I. The convention stops short of establishing specific criteria to be applied in granting or withholding permits. Instead it lists several considerations to be taken into account by national authorities in establishing criteria. These include the characteristics of the material (form, properties, toxicity, persistence, etc.), characteristics of the dumping site, and method of dumping (location, dilution and disposal, bottom conditions, etc.), and more general conditions. The last general consideration is most enlightening. It is the practical availability of alternative land-based methods of treatment, disposal, or elimination. This reflects an underlying ambivalent attitude toward ocean dumping and a recognition that the alternatives to ocean dumping may be too costly or may themselves be environmentally more damaging. With regard to materials not listed in Annexes I and II, a general permit is to be issued and records kept as to the nature of the dumped material, location, and method of dumping.

Certain limitations of the convention should be noted. It does not apply to incidental dumping from normal ship operations. It does not apply to marine sewage outfalls, such as are used on the U.S. West Coast, in which municipal sewage residuals are piped to sea. It does not cover wastes from exploiting and processing offshore seabed minerals (thus excluding the considerable wastes from oil drilling operations, and manganese nodule mining). It does not apply to military vessels. There is a saving clause permitting emergency dumping of blacklist materials, and also provision for dumping other materials if necessary for the safety of human life or vessels.

As noted, the specific criteria to be followed in issuing permits are left to the national authorities. The parties are to apply the provisions of the convention to their flag vessels, to all vessels loading in their territory for dumping, and to vessels believed to be dumping within their jurisdiction. Enforcement and penalties are left entirely to national governments. "Each Party will take in its territory appropriate measures to prevent and punish conduct in contravention of the provisions of this Convention."[4] With respect to the highly critical question of coastal state jurisdiction the convention defers to the Law of the Sea Conference.

Nothing in this Convention shall prejudice the codification and development of the law of the sea by the United Nations Conference on the Law of the Sea convened pursuant to Resolution 2750C (XXV) of the General Assembly of the United Nations nor the present or future claims and legal views of any State concerning the law of the sea and the nature and extent of coastal and flag state jurisdiction. The Contracting Parties agree to consult at a meeting to be convened by the Organisation after the Law of the Sea Conference, and in any case not later than 1976, with a view to defining the nature and extent of the right and the responsibility of a coastal state to apply the Convention in a zone adjacent to its coast.[5]

While these form the main provisions of the convention, they are better understood in the context of U.S. ocean dumping control activities. This is so for two reasons. First, the initiative for international control arose in the United States, and was simultaneous with the passage of U.S. legislation controlling dumping. Second, the convention leaves a major discretionary element to national authorities, and its effectiveness will be determined in large measure by the vigor with which national governments such as the United States act in this area.

The origin of U.S. action was a Presidential directive in 1970 to the Council on Environmental Quality to study ocean dumping. The subsequent CEQ report outlined the dimensions of U.S. ocean dumping and presented policy recommendations. The report stressed the need for preventive

---

[4] Article VII, 2.

[5] Almost all of the interpretive notes to the convention dealt with this statement, indicating the extremely sensitive nature of the jurisdictional question.

rather than remedial action. It concluded that dumping was not then a serious nationwide problem, but a national policy was needed to control expected growth and to minimize costly adjustments at a later date. It further suggested that international control over ocean dumping be considered at the forthcoming Stockholm Conference.

The resulting legislation, signed into law in October 1972, is structurally similar to the Ocean Dumping Convention. It includes a black list for which dumping is prohibited. Special and general permits are to be issued, although there is no attempt in the legislation to delineate a "grey list." As in the Ocean Dumping Convention, criteria for granting permits are not established in the legislation itself, but it does list considerations to be taken into account as the Environmental Protection Agency (EPA) formulates permit criteria. The considerations are somewhat less specific than those found in the ocean Dumping Convention, but do include the availability of alternative disposal methods: "Appropriate locations and methods of disposal and recycling, including land-based alternatives and the probable impact of requiring use of such alternative locations or methods on considerations affecting the public interest."

Control over dumping outside the jurisdiction of the United States—the three-mile territorial sea plus the nine-mile contiguous zone, to the extent that dumping in that zone affects the environment of territorial waters—is accomplished by regulating transport of material through territorial waters for eventual dumping. Thus reliance is placed on the internationally accepted right of states to control commerce proceeding from home ports, and, in accordance with U.S. military interests, there is no hint of sanctioning broad environmental zones. The legislation cannot be interpreted by others as a justification for unilaterally extending their ocean jurisdiction for environmental purposes. As expected, the domestic legislation departs from the Ocean Dumping Convention by explicitly establishing penalties (civil and criminal, with fines up to $50,000 for each violation), and setting forth enforcement and litigation procedures.

In accordance with the requirements of the legislation, the EPA issued interim regulations and criteria governing the issuance of permits in April and May 1973, and, following a period in which interested parties were invited to submit comments, published final regulations and criteria in October 1973. The criteria were deliberately constructed to be in harmony with the Ocean Dumping Convention. In August 1973, the United States ratified the Ocean Dumping Convention. Also, in June 1973, a bill was introduced to amend the domestic legislation to bring it into conformity with the Ocean Dumping Convention. The amendments were primarily of a technical nature. Thus the process of domestic implementation of the more general obligations of the multilateral convention is complete, and evaluation of the multilateral convention can be supported by reference to the domestic legislation and criteria established by the EPA.

EVALUATION

Chapter I set forth three basic areas for decision in establishing environmental control policies and argued that each decision had an economic dimension from which a criterion for evaluation could be extracted. How do the ocean dumping control measures fare in light of these criteria? The first area for decision concerns the extent of pollution abatement desired, or the environmental quality sought. The guiding economic principle is to equate marginal social costs of abatement to marginal social benefits from abatement (marginal social damages avoided). In broad outline, both the multilateral and domestic measures are in accordance with this principle, although the marginal principle is not explicit. There is no outright prohibition on all ocean dumping, nor is this found in a statement of intent. The Ocean Dumping Convention Preamble implicitly accepts the notion that the oceans have a natural, though limited, capacity to assimilate wastes.[6]

[6] In contrast to the goals of the 1972 Federal Water Pollution Control Act Amendments, which declare it a national goal that all discharge of pollutants

While the two measures fall short of explicit inclusion of the marginal principle, their provisions both permit and give limited encouragement to adherence. By classifying material according to potential damage, treating each separately, and emphasizing the importance of dumping site selection, the control measures allow discriminatory treatment of materials that is necessary for the marginal principle to obtain. The inclusion in both measures of the clause concerning availability or impact of alternative sites or disposal methods clearly introduces the real resource costs of curtailing ocean dumping. "It was agreed that alternative means of disposal to ocean dumping should be within some bounds of reason regarding costs";[7] The importance of this clause for economic rationality should be stressed. In a benefit cost calculation of an environmental control measure for one method of disposal, the only legitimate benchmark for calculating costs is the cost of alternative disposal methods.

Additional features of the measures and related materials can be cited. The technique of leaving to national authorities the job of establishing specific permit criteria allows for local differences in both damage and control cost functions. Universal criteria would not be consistent with local differences. The initial study done by the Council on Environmental Quality (CEQ) in 1970 devoted considerable effort to identifying alternative disposal methods and the costs associated with these methods. The U.S. legislation authorizes expenditures of up to $6 million annually in research, developing data on the effects of pollution on the marine environment and related economic considerations. Presumably, better data will emerge and assist in constructing damage functions. With regard to dump-

---

into navigable waterways be eliminated by 1985, with absolutely no statement regarding the costs of such action.

    [7] "Report of the U.S. delegation, reprinted in *Hearings on H.R. 5450 Before the Subcommittee on Fisheries and Wildlife Conservation and the Environment and the Subcommittee on Oceanography of the House Committee on Merchant Marine & Fisheries*, 93rd Cong., 1st Sess., Serial No. 93–14 (1973).

ing dredge spoils, which is administered by the Army Corps of Engineers, the U.S. legislation states that "Based upon an evaluation of the potential effect of a permit denial on navigation, economic and industrial development, and foreign and domestic commerce of the United States the Secretary (of the Army) shall make an independent determination of the need for dumping. The Secretary shall also make an independent determination as to other possible methods of disposal and as to the appropriate locations for the dumping."

All this indicates that the two measures have been written in a fashion such that they are not in conflict with the principle of marginal social costs equated with marginal social benefits. This does not guarantee least social cost waste disposal however. First, ocean dumping is a very small fraction of marine pollution—perhaps 10%—and a piecemeal approach, in which some sources of marine pollution are controlled according to the marginal principle, while other sources go unregulated, may not represent a least cost solution. For example, if it is established that the oceans have a natural capacity to assimilate wastes and render them harmless, and that this capacity is limited, then a fully rational environmental control policy would first control pollution sources for which there are inexpensive alternatives and move to the next least expensive source, and so on until the aggregate input of wastes was such that the marginal benefits from control were equated with the marginal costs for each source. The fragmented approach to marine pollution, and in particular the lack of international controls of any kind over land-based sources, preclude this comprehensive approach. It may be that the least-social-cost method for achieving ocean environmental quality goals will be control of land-based sources, but the partial approach, by pollution source, is incapable of achieving this.

Second, because of their partial nature, the measures may not respond to the transferability of wastes. For example, Ogilvie reports that many firms and communities in the United States have the option of shifting from the use of river outfalls to ocean dumping, and he cites a case in which a court order forcing the discontinuation of marine sewage outfalls by thirty-two New Jersey communities resulted in a diversion of these wastes to ocean dumping.[8]

The disposal of sewage sludge is another case in point. The initial CEQ report on ocean dumping identified incineration and land-fill as alternatives to ocean dumping.[9] Both are subject to creating environmental damage and the CEQ notes that current land-based operations are often not adequate to protect the environment. In its dumping permit application, New York City authorities listed reasons for not using alternatives, such as land-fill, recycling for agricultural use, incineration, and injection into wells. Each of these alternatives was stated to be more costly than ocean dumping and each was associated with other environmental damages, including ground-water contamination and atmospheric pollution.

In order for the Ocean Dumping Convention and related legislation on the national level to contribute toward improving efficiency in waste disposal, recognizing that wastes can and will be shunted from one disposal site to another, and from one environmental medium to another, it will be necessary for national governments to have comprehensive and integrated waste disposal policies. Moreover, these integrated waste disposal policies must incorporate not only the financial but also the environmental costs (damages) associated with alternative disposal sites and mediums. Ogilvie is pessimistic on this score, stating that in the United States the method of cost-benefit used has included private costs, but has not systematically included social costs and benefits, thus effectively discounting environmental damages.[10] Internationally there is little reason to be optimistic, as most countries have less comprehensive programs for waste disposal and environmental quality than does the United States.

[8] P. Ogilvie, "Ocean Dumping and the EPA," May 1974, unpublished.

[9] Also pipeline disposal through marine outfalls and use of sludge as a soil conditioner.

[10] Ogilvie, "Ocean Dumping and the EPA," p. 6.

If the Ocean Dumping Convention is seriously implemented abroad, the results must be closely monitored to avoid a mere *diversion* of wastes from one site or medium to another, involving perhaps higher private and environmental costs.

In summary, both the multinational and domestic dumping control instruments permit the marginal principle to obtain, but there are serious grounds for believing that it will not obtain in practice.

The second major area for decision in formulating environmental controls involves the choice of instruments or techniques for achieving the quality goals that have been established.[11] As discussed in Chapter I, the related economic criterion was choosing instruments that minimize the real resource cost of achieving the environmental quality objectives. In turn, cost minimization involves internalizing externality costs and closing the distance between private and social costs, minimizing enforcement costs and providing incentive for innovation in abatement technology, and effectively distinguishing between high and low alternative abatement cost pollution sources.

The Ocean Dumping Convention and U.S. domestic legislation has chosen a set of instruments that is essentially prohibitory/regulatory in nature, in contrast to tax/subsidy or environmental usage certificate schemes that work indirectly through the price system. Both a regulatory scheme involving standards and permits and a tax scheme working through the price mechanism are capable of forcing the internalization of externalities, and bringing private prices into alignment with social costs.[12] For example, a tax on the disposal of chemical effluent in the oceans and a requirement to pretreat wastes before dumping would both increase production costs and, presumably, increase product prices so that they more nearly

[11] For a more detailed discussion of this issue, see C. Pearson. "Extracting Rent From Ocean Resources: Discussion of a Neglected Source," *Ocean Development & International Law Journal* 1, no. 3 (1973).

[12] For convenience we shall only discuss a tax system, recognizing that the same basic conclusions hold for subsidy and environmental usage certificate schemes.

approximated the full private and social (environmental) marginal costs of production.

Additionally, a regulatory scheme could be administered as efficiently as a tax system, if the authorities had full knowledge of the following:

—differences in alternative (private) disposal costs among potential ocean dumpers;
—differences in private costs of ocean dumping among potential dumpers;
—differences in alternative environmental disposal costs among ocean dumpers;
—differences in recycling opportunities among ocean dumpers;

and if they acted on this knowledge by issuing permits to those potential dumpers who face the highest relative private and environmental costs from using alternatives, and who have least opportunity for recycling, and denied permits to those potential dumpers who face low alternative disposal costs and for whom recycling material is most easily accomplished. Clearly, the informational requirements for the permit-granting authority are large and expensive. Nor can one easily shift the cost of acquiring this information on to the dumpers, as is attempted in the U.S. legislation and subsequent EPA regulations. Although permit applicants are obliged to make statements why alternatives are not available or feasible, there is no way to check the accuracy of the information unless the government has independent knowledge and expertise in the area. Naturally, ocean dumping applicants will have every incentive to exaggerate the costs of alternative disposal or recycling methods.[13]

In contrast, a tax scheme that placed charges on ocean dumping at the appropriate rate to equate marginal costs and marginal benefits would automatically force individual potential dumpers to consider less expensive alternatives, including recycling. Presumably, they have much more complete

[13] Ogilvie reports that these statements are incomplete, and without specific cost data regarding alternatives. This situation is even less promising with regard to dredge spoils. In this case the Army Corps of Engineers is both the dumper and the regulator.

data on their individual cost alternatives, and the tax would automatically make the distinctions listed above between dumpers without obliging the environmental authorities to have this full set of data. Thus higher environmental quality could be attained for an equal expenditure of real resources. Further, a tax on ocean dumping that is capable of discriminating among dumpers on the basis of alternative costs would reduce the lobbying efforts of individual dumpers and the consequent potential for excessive dumping or "favoritism."

At the same time, some cautions are in order. First, the tax scheme would not relieve the authorities of the need to make decisions regarding the overall marine quality objectives, and this necessarily requires data on overall abatement cost functions as well as benefit (damage) functions. Second, a tax system does not eliminate the danger of diverting waste flows into other mediums, as described earlier. It can be argued that internationally, as environmental programs are considerably less than comprehensive, a regulatory/permit system has greater flexibility in avoiding such diversions. Finally, the great diversity of wastes entering the ocean through dumping, and the diversity of damages depending on ocean dumping site location create serious practical problems. The tax charge would have to be specific to both the type of waste and the site location to be efficient. Also the rate of tax for a particular type of waste and location would be difficult to set. The proliferation of rates might be a very real obstacle. The problem, of course, is also present in the current regulatory/permit system, as the authorities must explicitly or implicitly account for different type wastes and different dumping locations.

Under these circumstances perhaps the loss of efficiency in choosing the regulatory instrument, as was done in the Ocean Dumping Convention and the U.S. legislation, is not excessive and can be minimized as the governmental agencies improve their knowledge and expertise on the private and environmental costs of alternatives to ocean dumping. At a minimum, however, the authorities should demand the highest possible quality statements from permit applicants, to improve their data base for decisions.

Before concluding this discussion of the efficiency of the instruments chosen to implement ocean dumping objectives, two other points should be noted. First, to the extent that ocean dumpers are not private firms, it is not certain that externalities are being effectively internalized. Consider municipal sewage sludge disposal and the higher costs associated with implementation of ocean dumping measures. Industrial users of municipal systems are most often charged on the basis of property values and metered water use and not on waste loads. Additionally, municipal treatment plants are subvented by the federal government. Therefore, additional costs for abatement brought about by restrictions on ocean dumping will be distributed to industrial users according to property values and water use, not according to waste loads, and to the public through general taxation. These costs will not find their way into relative product prices and will not bring market prices into alignment with social costs.[14]

Second, the current system, and in particular the criteria developed by the EPA for granting permits for materials requiring special care (227.31 and 227.71, including certain heavy metals, organosilicon compounds, petrochemical, etc.), may discourage innovation and technological improvement in pollution abatement. Essentially, the EPA has established maximum permissible concentrations of these wastes in receiving waters—1% of a concentration shown to be toxic to appropriate marine organisms. This means that a dumper who has met this standard either by dilution or by pretreatment is not offered any additional incentive to further reduce waste loads and, unless he has an opportunity to meet this standard through a less expensive method, will presumably cease to look for better methods of abatement or recycling.

Chapter I identified a third area for decision in the formation of environmental control policies, whether to accept or

[14] Similarly, dredging is done by the Corps of Engineers, and additional costs from restrictions on dumping dredge spoils will be borne by the taxpayer.

modify the change in welfare distribution consequent to the control measure. That any measure to control marine pollution that goes beyond mere exhortation will improve the welfare of certain groups and deteriorate the relative and perhaps absolute welfare of other groups is clear. Full investigation of the distributional effects would involve identifying groups and countries and measuring their gains and losses. Data limitations and the absence of implementing legislation in most countries preclude this fine analysis for ocean dumping. Instead, we offer some more speculative remarks on the likely direction of change.

The welfare distributional issue in ocean dumping can be broken into four components; internal shifts, external (international) shifts, inter-temporal redistribution, and the question of rent. Internally, the increased costs associated with restrictions on ocean dumping will be borne as follows by three groups, taxpayers, consumers, and productive factors.[15] The incidence of costs as between taxpayers and the other two groups depends on three factors; the degree to which the government is the ocean dumper (as, for example, in the United States as the Army Corps of Engineers performs its dredging functions in clearing harbors and channels for navigation), the amount of assistance given by government to the private sector for pollution abatement expenditures, and the magnitude of administrative and enforcement costs falling on the government authorities. For example, if the Corps obliges itself to use more expensive means of disposing of polluted dredge spoils, the additional costs will be passed along through the tax system.[16] Also, if the private sector is limited in ocean dumping and forced to turn to higher cost alternatives, part of the cost will still be absorbed by government, to the extent that it subvents general pollution abatement expenditures in the private sector. The widespread use of government assistance, including subsidized capital costs and tax advantages, suggests that not all of the additional cost

[15] One individual can simultaneously belong to each group.

[16] Municipalities may be obliged to provide sites for diking activities and may pass this cost along to shippers through increased port charges.

to industry will be lodged there. Also, if municipalities are obliged to turn to higher cost alternatives for disposing of sewage sludge and solid wastes, the general tax burden will increase. Finally, the taxpayer will pay certain administrative and enforcement costs, including research and monitoring of disposal sites. In this regard, proposed EPA regulations concerning dumping site management require dumpers to assume some financial cost of monitoring. It has been suggested that monitoring costs, estimated to be up to $1.5 million per dump site, may be sufficient to discourage marginal dumpers—a modest move toward the tax system for ocean dumping suggested earlier.

The portion of cost increases not assumed by taxpayers through the government will be split between consumers in the form of higher prices for those products for which production costs, including waste disposal, have increased, and productive factors in the form of lower wages or profits. The exact split will be determined by the market structure of the industries affected and, specifically, the ability of firms to pass along price increases. The cost increases arising from controls on ocean dumping are apt to be small relative to total pollution control costs and, especially, the costs associated with the 1972 Water Pollution Control Act Amendments, and, therefore, will not be very noticeable in product prices. Nor is it likely that the ocean dumping regulations will of themselves force plant closings and unemployment. A reading of the testimony and literature suggests that the sharpest impact may be felt by the New York City area, which currently dumps 5½ million cubic yards of sewage sludge per year 12 miles out to sea and is expected to dump 18 million cubic yards by 1980.[17] If barged 70 miles out, as suggested by the EPA, the incremental cost for sewage sludge alone in the New York City area might be $90 million for the year 1980. A very rough estimate of the annual cost of complying with U.S. ocean dumping legislation, including enforcement and monitoring costs, might be $200 to 300 million by 1980. There

[17] *Christian Science Monitor*, April 10, 1974.

does not appear to be any specific plan for compensating those who bear the increased cost burden, beyond the normal aids by the federal government to industry and to municipalities for pollution abatement. In practice, however, assistance may well be given by stretching out the timetable for curtailing dumping and relaxing standards when the burden appears to be "unreasonable."

The domestic beneficiaries of ocean dumping control are difficult to identify. Fish and shellfish industries and their customers, tourist and recreational users of the ocean, shorefront property owners, environmentalists, who attach intrinsic value to the marine environment, will of course be accorded increased welfare, either monetary, health, or psychic, but further classification is impossible. In any event, the benefits will be widespread—over two-thirds of the population lives within 50 miles of the coast—and the benefits will not be concentrated in a small number of individuals.[18]

It is equally difficult to be specific about the international distributional consequences. In general, we can say that countries that have low cost alternatives to ocean dumping, and that are major beneficial users of other ocean resources threatened by marine pollution such as tourism and fisheries, will gain the most, while the relative (and perhaps absolute) welfare of countries that are faced with high cost alternatives and that use the waste disposal capacity of the oceans more extensively than its other services, will decline. Even this, however, must be qualified. The global ocean dumping convention is not specific with regard to obligations of members, aside from the blacklist items, and therefore each country is able to design implementing legislation on the basis of its own national cost-benefit calculus. This suggests that no individual country will design legislation to make itself worse off—recalling the proposition developed earlier that a necessary condition for a negotiated international environmental control instrument was that all parties be made no worse off.

---

[18] In this connection see the discussion of benefits from the Prevention of Pollution from Ships Convention, below.

Additionally, as a factual matter, most of the identifiable costs from ocean dumping accrue to the dumping state—therefore, most of the benefits from controlling dumping also accrue to that state. While there are regional instances where mutual reciprocal externalities are strong, such as in the Mediterranean and the North Sea area, a large proportion of the external costs from dumping are internalized to the dumping country.

Stated in somewhat different form, the international distributional question and related constraints did not dominate the negotiations for the Ocean Dumping Convention for three reasons. First, the convention is not specific with respect to implementing legislation, leaving each country free to establish regulations on the basis of its own benefit/cost calculations. Second, the amount of external costs from ocean dumping and flowing among countries is small relative to external costs absorbed within countries, and, therefore, the international distributional question is less important. Finally, it appears that the architects of the agreement had more than a narrow national welfare perspective in mind and, indeed, had some attachment to a global welfare concept.

The only specific international policy to modify the distributional effects of the convention is found in Appendix III (Annex 3 of Final Act), and by reference therein, Article 9. Appendix III was inserted as a compromise following a request by Ghana for the establishment of an international compensation fund to assist developing countries with the costs of implementing the convention. Appendix III and Article 9 make no firm commitment of funds, but simply state that the parties will promote, through international organizations, support for training, monitoring, and costs associated with alternatives to ocean dumping.

What may eventually prove to be the most significant distributional consequence of measures to limit marine pollution generally, and ocean dumping specifically, is the intertemporal redistribution of welfare. When considering the use and abuse of environmental resources it is useful to think in terms of a dynamic stock—flow relationship. The stock of environmental resources, adjusted for quality changes, at any point in time yields a flow of services in the form of waste assimilative capacity—the ability to absorb and render harmless wastes. If waste disposal demands do not exceed this capacity, the stock of environmental resources remains of constant quality over time. However, if demands for waste disposal exceed assimilative capacity, the quality adjusted stock diminishes over time and the flow rate of excess demand determines the change in stock per unit time according to the dynamic accounting relations that a net flow equals change in stock per unit time.

Put less formally, excessive use of the oceans for waste disposal impairs the quality of the oceans and reduces the real resources, natural and man-made, available to subsequent generations, and therefore reduces their welfare while adding to ours. The present generation is consuming "environmental capital" and not conserving it for the future. The literature on cost-benefit analysis is replete with discussions as to how one should properly value costs and benefits occurring in the future. There is general agreement that future costs and benefits should be discounted to the present to determine their present value or worth, but the rate of discount is a wide-open controversy. There is some support that the discount rate should reflect the social time preference for present consumption over future consumption, but this is impossible to measure empirically and excludes from the calculus the preferences of future generations. Moreover, the social time preference for one country or group will be significantly different from that for other groups, depending on income levels, values, and so forth.

With respect to marine environment, then, the situation of uncontrolled pollution is one in which there is an involuntary transfer of welfare from the future to the current generation. Effective marine pollution control instruments will limit or possibly reverse this transfer. The question of how to discount the costs passed forward by pollution or the benefits conferred by marine pollution abatement can perhaps be sidestepped.[19] A persuasive argument can be made that two of the major economic services provided by the ocean and threatened by pollution will increase in relative and absolute value over time. Certainly, there is evidence that recreation and related amenities is an income elastic service in relatively constant supply. This will result in increasing the absolute and relative value of ocean-related recreational services. Also, the oceans presently constitute a very major direct and indirect source of global food supplies. World fisheries catch was almost 8% of world production of cereal grains in 1968 (by volume) and, more importantly, as a source of protein equaled 13% of total meat, milk, and eggs production. Furthermore, world cereal grains production increased about 50% from 1955 to 1968, while the fish catch increased by 120% during the same period.[20]

Rising world population and increased pressure on traditional sources of food supplies will also force up the absolute and relative value of the oceans as a source of food. Consequently, we can argue that the expected increase in the value of the beneficial services provided by the oceans is sufficiently large to offset any reasonable rate of social time preference for present over future consumption, and, therefore, we are fully justified in establishing the current quality of the marina environment as a minimum objective.

The final distributional issue to be noted concerns rent and ownership.[21] Assuming that there is some level of ocean dumping that does not degrade the marine environment, and assuming, quite reasonably, that the alternative to certain types of ocean dumping are more expensive, a regulatory permit system for dumping, such as is contemplated in the

[19] While the author has no problem with the rationale for discounting future benefits and costs in customary cost-benefit analysis, discounting future environmental damages seems less justified if only because the uncertainty regarding long-run environmental effects has been a dismal history of continually underestimating ultimate damages.

[20] Fish catch equals about 1/8 lb. per person per day worldwide average.

[21] For elaboration, see Pearson, "Extracting Rent from Ocean Resources."

Ocean Dumping Convention and in U.S. legislation, confers an economically valuable right to the dumper. If the oceans were under national or international ownership, the authorities could collect a rental payment for the assimilative service currently provided free to dumpers.

Indeed, the concept of ocean resources as the common heritage of mankind does suggest some ownership rights. Current discussions concerning the distribution of revenues from mining nodules on the deep seabed floor center on this question. "Although nodules and assimilative capacity are vastly different types of resources, and the orderly exploitation of each encounters different sets of problems, there seems to be little difference in principle between attempts to extract income for the benefit of mankind from the two. In both cases, if international ownership can be asserted, the free transfer of valuable rights is avoided, and rental income accrues to the owner."

The conclusion, then, is that the current ocean dumping regime is one in which "ocean dumpers are appropriating to themselves the rights to an environmental service without payment to the putative owners."[22] A welfare transfer is being made from mankind to dumpers, and an appropriate tax on ocean dumping might both improve the allocational efficiency of ocean environment resources, as described earlier, and also provide a substantial rental income.

[22] Ibid., p. 236.

IV.

INTERNATIONAL CONVENTION FOR THE PREVENTION OF POLLUTION FROM SHIPS

BACKGROUND

While the convention covers virtually all aspects of pollution from ships, its most important features deal with oil pollution and, in particular pollution from oil tankers. Accordingly, it is useful to present some background data on the amounts and sources of marine oil pollution. Table 7 contains this information.

Table 7 shows that approximately 43% of marine oil pollution arises from marine as opposed to land-based sources. Of this 43%, routine tanker operations contribute about 60% and tanker accidents another 8% so that 30% of all marine oil pollution is accounted for by tankers, and the annual amount is over 1 million metric tons per year. Addi-

TABLE 7. ESTIMATED SOURCES AND QUANTITIES OF OIL POLLUTION OF THE OCEANS

	Metric tons	%
Tanker operations		
LOT cleaning/ballasting[a]	84,499	2.4
Non-LOT cleaning/ballasting	455,708	13.2
Product tankers using shore reception facilities	19,492	0.6
Product tankers *not* using shore reception facilities	63,832	1.9
Ore/bulk/oil carriers cleaning and ballasting	119,543	3.4
Additional cleaning and disposal prior to drydocking	91,895	2.7
Tanker bilges	9,573	0.3
Tanker barges	12,787	0.4
Terminal operations	31,933	0.9
	889,262	25.8

TABLE 7. Continued

Other ship operations		
Bunkers	9,055	0.3
Bilges, cleaning, ballasting, etc.	292,481	8.5
	301,536	8.8
Vessel Accidents		
Tankers	104,268	3.0
Tank barges	19,803	0.6
All other vessels	48,972	1.4
	173,043	5.0
Offshore activities		
Offshore drilling	118,126	3.4
	118,126	3.4
Non-marine operations and accidents		
Refinery-petrochemical plant waste oils	195,402	5.7
Industrial machinery waste oil	718,468	20.8
Automotive waste oil	1,034,588	29.9
Pipelines	25,574	0.7
	1,974,032	57.1
Overall total	3,455,999	100.0

Source: Charter and Porricelli, "Quantitative Estimates of Petroleum to the Oceans."

[a]LOT—Load on Top, a technique in which oily water ballast is collected in slop tanks, with the heavier seawater settling to the bottom and being released. Fresh oil is then loaded directly on the oil residue in the slop tanks.

tionally, IMCO estimates with unchanged procedures, *marine source* oil pollution could increase 300% by the end of the century. Consequently, the convention is addressing a very major source of marine pollution to which its provisions concerning tanker operations are central.

Note that the data in Table 7 do not include hydrocarbon fallout from the atmosphere. Total gaseous emissions of volatile oil products are estimated to be 25 million tons per year.[1] No estimates of the amount that reaches the oceans are available.

To understand the convention it is useful to briefly describe how routine tanker operations result in oil spillage and the various ways in which spillage can be reduced. Operational oil spillage occurs as a result of ballasting, tankwashings, and terminal operations. Ballasting is the process of taking aboard seawater for additional weight for stability and safety for return voyages to loading ports. Without adequate ballast or cargo, tankers would be unmaneuverable and would break up in heavy seas. Ballast levels are from 45% to 60% of full load displacement for large tankers. When ballast water is pumped directly into cargo tanks it mixes with oil residues that remain after unloading. When pumped out again in the vicinity of the loading port the oily mixture contributes to marine oil pollution. The amount of oil pollution from de-ballasting can be large; tank cleaning and ballasting operations together amount to 540,000 metric tons of marine oil pollution.

There are three major methods for limiting pollution from ballasting operations; segregated ballasting, load on top (LOT), and onshore reception facilities. Segregated ballasting involves separate tanks for cargo and for ballast water, thus keeping the two physically segregated. It is important to note that this method automatically prevents contamination of ballast water and is not dependent on human judgment and possible error. Segregated ballasting may be accomplished with either single-skinned vessels, in which the tank hull is also the vessel hull, or with double-skinned hulls in which the ballast tanks are in part the space between the cargo hull and the vessel hull. LOT is a method by which oily ballast water is collected in slop tanks. The heavier sea water settles and is decanted and a fresh load is taken 'on top' of the remaining

---

[1] International Maritime Consultative Organization (IMCO), *Report of Study No. VI, The Environmental and Financial Consequences of Oil Pollution.* U.K. Dept. of Trade and Industry, 1973.

oil. LOT is not effective for short hauls, or in heavy seas which prevent settling. Additionally, the separation may not be complete and some oil is discharged during the decanting process. It is subject to human failures.[2] As implied in the name, onshore reception facilities involve retention of oily residue on board until it is transferred to a shore facility for separation or disposal.

Tank washings are a second source of marine oil pollution from routine tanker operations. Tanks are washed periodically to prevent oil residue build-up, when the cargo changes from one oil product or grade to another, and before dry-docking for repairs and maintenance. Onshore reception facilities for polluted tank washings are the major control method. Terminal operations spillage is that which occurs during loading and unloading—leaks in couplings, overflows, and so forth.

CONVENTION PROVISIONS[3]

In contrast to the Ocean Dumping Convention, this convention is a complicated document that is much more specific in establishing construction and operating regulations. The convention consists of general provisions, Annexes I and II, which are mandatory, and Annexes III, IV, and V, which are optional. The general provisions discuss application, procedures to be followed for violations, certificate and inspection regulations, reporting, dispute settlements, amendment procedures, and so forth. Dumping and pollution resulting from exploiting seabed minerals are excluded. Military vessels are excluded. Violations are subject to flag states' sanctions or, if the violation is within the jurisdiction of a state, the sanctions of that state. Vessels are required to hold valid certificates verifying compliance with construction and equipment stan-

---

[2] A fourth method has been proposed in which oil and ballast water are kept separate within a tank by using a flexible membrane. This method is not yet technologically feasible.

[3] For a summary of the convention provisions, see W. Benkert and D. Williams, "The Impact of the 1973 IMCO Convention on the Maritime Industry," *Marine Technology* (January 1974).

dards. Certificates are subject to inspection by port states within their jurisdiction, and vessels are also subject to inspection if a violation is suspected.

Annex I deals with oil pollution and is mandatory. It is concerned with both oil pollution from accidents and routine operations, and covers both tankers and all other vessels. For routine operations of tankers it specifies two major types of requirements—oil discharge limits, and construction and equipment regulations. The discharge limit is 60 liters of oil per mile, and not to exceed 1/15,000 cargo capacity for existing tankers and 1/30,000 cargo capacity for new tankers. Discharge can only take place while underway and more than fifty miles from land, and is completely prohibited in certain areas—the Mediterranean, Baltic, Black, and Red Seas, and the Persian Gulf and Sea of Oman. The very important construction and equipment requirement is for segregated ballast tanks for new tankers of 70,000 dead weight tons and above. Further requirements include slop tanks for collecting tank washings and an oil discharge monitoring system that measures, records, and regulates the discharge of oil wastes. These last two do not initially apply to existing tankers, and if monitoring systems are not available, the requirement can be waived. Contracting parties undertake to provide onshore reception facilities for oil residues and wastes from both tankers and other vessels.

In addition to these provisions for reducing routine oil discharge from tankers (and provisions concerning oil pollution from other vessels), Annex I contains provisions to limit oil pollution from accidents. These include limits on tank size, arrangement of cargo tanks, and structural strength for surviving accident damages.

Annex II, also mandatory, deals with other noxious liquid substances. The Annex provides four categories of noxious substances, ranging from minimum to maximum damage potential, and establishes separate discharge requirements for each in terms of rates, location, retention, and so forth.[4]

[4] Classification of substances by GESAMP.

Again, special areas are delimited for stricter standards, and shore reception facilities are to be provided. Governments are responsible for issuing design and equipment regulations to minimize accidental pollution.

Annex III, IV, and V are concerned with containerized substances, ship sewage discharges, and ship garbage, respectively. They are optional and of far less overall significance than Annexes I and II. Moreover, many of the provisions are left to governments for details, or are subject to long delays before coming into force.

ANALYSIS

From the perspective of economic analysis, the convention is a somewhat curious document. In contrast to the Ocean Dumping Convention, there are no references explicit or implicit to the economic benefits to be gained from reducing marine pollution, or the economic costs associated with implementing the convention provisions. Indeed, the statement of purpose declares as the goal "the complete elimination of intentional pollution of the marine environment by oil and other harmful substances and the minimization of accidental discharge of such substances." This is, of course, weaker than the original objective set by the IMCO Assembly, to achieve "by 1975, if possible, but certainly by the end of the decade . . . the complete elimination of the willful and intentional pollution of the sea by oil and noxious substances other than oil."[5]

The purpose of the convention and supporting provisions stands in sharp contrast to the preparatory work conducted by IMCO, in which discussion of the economic costs and benefits of the proposed regulations were pervasive. In preparation, IMCO commissioned a series of nine background studies among member countries to determine the cost and effectiveness and expected benefits from control-

[5] Quoted by Hang-Sheng Cheng in "Is Compulsory Segregated Ballasting Needed and Justified for Reducing Pollution of the Sea?" U.S. Treasury, mimeo. (1973), p. 7. Note that this was later modified to read harmful discharges, rather than discharges as such.

ling ship pollution. These included studies of the cost and effectiveness of the major control instruments for oil pollution mentioned earlier—segregated ballasting, load on top, onshore reception facilities, and flexible membranes—and cost/effectiveness studies for controlling sewage, garbage, and other noxious wastes. Finally, IMCO designated the United Kingdom as lead country to study the environmental and financial consequences of oil pollution from ships (Study VI), in an obvious effort to develop data on damage functions and, hence, benefits to be derived from abatement of marine oil pollution.

Moreover, the concern for the costs and effectiveness of the convention was not confined to IMCO. The U.S. Treasury developed a preliminary cost-benefit analysis of segregated ballasting (to be discussed presently). In Hearings prior to the London Conference, the draft convention was discussed from the perspective of additional costs of segregated ballast tanks and the double-bottom requirement. The Coast Guard prepared a comprehensive study of the cost effectiveness of segregated ballasting with single and double hulls for various tanker sizes. The official U.S. position supported segregated ballasting and the requirement for double bottoms.

Too much should not be made of the concern for costs and benefits that surrounded the preparation of the convention and the absence of any reference to economic considerations in the document itself. As was suggested earlier, the first major question for decision in formulating environmental controls either nationally or internationally is determining the environmental quality objective, or, conversely, the pollution abatement objective. Theoretically, this should involve estimating abatement cost and pollution damage functions and setting objectives to equate marginal costs with marginal benefits (damages avoided). It is apparent, however, that this guideline had to be sacrificed as it was not possible to construct damage functions for marine oil pollution that were even minimally acceptable. As a result, the participants were forced to beg the question of optimal abatement levels and make a gross judgment that routine oil pollution should be sharply limited, but that some abatement costs were prohibitive and could not be contemplated. For example, it was generally agreed that the cost of refitting existing tankers to segregated ballasting would be excessive and this option was not considered. Having concluded this, the central question became one of instruments: which type control would be most cost effective in limiting routine oil pollution, rather than "are the marginal costs of abatement equal to the marginal benefits?" Having investigated the cost-effectiveness question prior to the conference, the final document could avoid reference both to cost/benefit and cost effectiveness; the former question being unanswered and the answer to the latter question implicit in the major control instrument actually specified—segregated ballasting.

Before turning to an examination of the selection of abatement control instruments, it is useful to note why it was impossible to establish damage estimates that had minimal support among participants. The main effort that was undertaken was done by the Programs Analysis Unit of the Department of Trade and Industry of the U.K. government, entitled "The Environmental and Financial Consequences of Oil Pollution from Ships."[6] The authors were faced with a formidable task. The list of uncertainties is long—sources and amounts of oil, dilution, distribution and dispersal, chemical changes, effects on marine biota, converting physical effects into economic costs. At each stage there seems to be considerable professional controversy.

However, making allowances for the formidable nature of the task, the report is disturbing. In tone and detail it consistently plays down or underestimates the economic damages done by oil pollution. Examples can be cited. On a general level, damages are broken into two categories, "economic costs" and "welfare reductions," to correspond to those that involve market transactions and those that do not. Even the choice of terms seems unfortunate; market and

[6] IMCO Study VI.

nonmarket transactions both involve welfare changes and, given a reasonable interpretation of utility functions, economic costs. Because damage costs that do not pass through markets are inherently difficult to quantify and because by definition the study did not consider these economic costs, there was a discernible tendency to slight or ignore them. In addition, conclusions were drawn from a lack of contrary evidence. For example, the report acknowledges at one point: "At the present time there is insufficient knowledge of the behavior of marine stocks to allow the identification and quantification of the effects of oil pollution" (4.11), but at a different point: "Unless the effects are delayed or cumulative, and we have no reason to believe them to be, we can regard the absence of significant damage to fish stocks as evidence that no significant change in their food has occurred and that there are negligible economic consequences up to this point in time. The only economic effects of oil pollution that can be quantified are those occurring during major incidents" (4.44).

This is a tricky statement. First, the purpose of the study is precisely to look at incremental damages, and the focus here is on past damages. Second, there may be no reason to believe effects to be cumulative or delayed, but there may be no reason not to believe this either, and one has a choice of assumptions. Third, the statement should note the absence of *evidence* showing damage to fish stocks and not the absence of significant damage to fish stocks.

To summarize, the initial U.S. reaction to the report was: "From the foregoing it appears that the authors of the report evaluated oil pollution as harmful only when its effects were: (a) obvious, (b) widespread, (c) visible, (d) critical, (e) direct. The harmful effects of oil pollution need to be evaluated not only as indicated above, but also with respect to harmful effects which are: (a) subtle, (b) localized, (c) invisible, (d) indirect, (e) long term."[7]

---

[7] Preliminary comments submitted by the United States on IMCO Study VI.

The sobering conclusion is that damage assessments are notoriously difficult and subject to controversy. In such a situation much depends on who is selected to make the analysis. In this case the study was done under the auspices of the Ministry of Trade and Industry, a department with strong interests in low-cost ocean transport of industrial raw materials, by a country which is heavily dependent on imported petroleum for industrial output.[8]

Having essentially bypassed the difficult question of formulating benefit functions for the purpose of establishing optimal pollution abatement levels, preparatory work for the conference could concentrate on the second broad area for decision in formulating environmental control policy— selecting instruments to achieve environmental quality objectives. While the majority of the preparatory analytical studies focused on alternative technologies, such as segregated ballasting and LOT, it is important to recognize the broader spectrum of choices that was present. A sequence of choices was involved: first, the question of altering the legal regime so that shippers would be fully liable for damages and could either compensate or take preventive action; second, if this were rejected, to establish oil discharge standards or to require design and equipment standards; third, if design and equipment standards were selected, to choose between alternative design/equipment technologies; and, finally, if segregated ballasting was selected as the preferred design/ equipment, to choose between double-bottom or single-bottom segregated ballasting.

Each of these choices can be evaluated according to the criterion suggested in Chapter I—selecting instruments that will minimize the real resource costs of attaining objectives. In turn, the dimensions of this criterion are the internalization of externalities, the minimization of enforcement costs, the

---

[8] Echoes of the same issue can be found in a report by Jack Anderson, who states that a warning about cancer from marine oil pollution was deleted from a restricted draft study by the National Academy of Sciences, and who notes that scientists from major oil companies helped prepare the report. *The Washington Post,* June 1, 1974.

incentive for innovation, and the effective distinguishing between high and low abatement cost pollution sources. We start our review with the question of strengthening the legal regime so that shippers would be liable for damages.

From an abstract and simplified viewpoint, this would offer significant advantages. Shippers could choose between payment for damages or preventive measures on the basis of least cost. Compensation payments or prevention measures would be internalized to shippers and their customers, and the social cost of oil transport would be more nearly reflected in product prices. An economic incentive would be present to innovate in pollution abatement and thus reduce shipping costs. Each shipper could choose on the basis of his own cost circumstances whether to abate or pay and how to abate so that cost differences among shippers would be respected.[9]

More realistically, the assignment of liability for damages to shippers would probably not function effectively. With regard to routine oil discharges, the classic failures of private bargaining would be present. The number of damaged parties is large, the physical pathways of marine oil pollution are complex, and the sources of oil pollution are difficult to identify. The transactions costs, including aggregating the interests of damaged parties, and the costs of negotiating settlements and enforcing contracts are prohibitive. The case for liability for major accidental oil spills near coastlines is somewhat better, but is still very weak. Certainly, shippers can be charged for cleanup operations, but the amounts paid may be only indirectly related to damages suffered.[10] More importantly, there does not seem to be any practical method for indemnifying indirectly damaged parties, including local community businesses, bathers who incur costs while seeking cleaner but more distant beaches, future generations for

[9] The scheme could be implemented in conjunction with an internationally assessed tax on oil discharged in the oceans, as suggested in the ocean dumping case. This would then approach an effluent/emission charges system, preserve theoretical advantages, and avoid some of the disadvantages listed above.

[10] IMCO VI, 4.29, 4.30.

possible loss of fish resources, and so forth. Without accurate identification and awareness of those who suffer damages, it is unlikely that damage claims presented to shippers will reflect true damages.[11]

In this connection, it should be noted that the 1971 International Convention on the Establishment of an International Fund for Compensation for Oil Pollution Damages fails to meet the primary economic efficiency test. The fund is set up so that beyond certain minimums, shippers are relieved of damage compensation payments, and payments to the fund made by oil importers are proportional to tonnage imported. Damage costs are not internalized to shippers, and the incentive to minimize spills is accordingly reduced.[12]

Having rejected reliance on shippers' liability as the main control instrument for routine oil pollution, the next question involved a choice between design and equipment standards and oil discharge standards. The convention includes both segregated ballasting and LOT facilities and discharge standards of 1/30,000 ships cargo and a discharge rate no more than 60 liters of oil per mile. Both approaches meet the test of internalizing externality costs and, to the extent that the segregated ballasting/LOT requirements are different for large and small tankers and for new and existing tankers, there is an attempt to distinguish between high and low abatement cost pollution sources.

The advantage of a discharge standard alone, without a

[11] This is even more true when one recognizes that an oil spill will result in net damages that are different than gross damages because of second round welfare charges. For example, the hotel owner at resort community A will have gross losses from patronage losses, but hotels in resorts B and C may increase occupancy rates and profits as tourists avoid the polluted beach at A. The hotel owner at A would present a claim for his gross damage, not the net damage to society. For a discussion of current recovery rights under U.S. law, see J. Sweeney, "Private Damages from Oil Spills in a Marine Environment," in *Assessing the Social Impacts of Oil Spills,* Proceedings of an Invitational Symposium Co-Sponsored by The Institute for Man and Science, and the U.S. Environmental Protection Agency, Rensselaerville, N.Y. (1973).

[12] Accidentally released oil is, of course, a loss and an incentive for safe tanker construction and operation. The fund no doubt reflects concern for bankruptcy and nonpayment.

design/equipment standard, is that it would permit shippers to select the least cost method of control—segregated ballasting, load on top, shipboard retention with shore facilities, or whatever. By stipulating segregated ballasting for new ships above 70,000 tons, however, the convention, in effect, makes the discharge standard redundant for these vessels (except tank washing discharges) and *requires* the use of a particular technology. The economic efficiency of this requirement has been challenged. In an interesting study prepared for the Treasury Department, Hang-Sheng Cheng has calculated that the *incremental* benefit cost ratio from requiring segregated ballasting might be exceedingly low. His estimate of incremental benefits to the United States for 1980 from segregated ballasting might be $68,000, and incremental costs might be $120,000,000, or a B/C ratio of 0.0005 (single-bottom).[13] It should be immediately noted that his cost and benefit data are open to question and that benefits were restricted to commercial fishing, navigation, and seashore recreation for which there was a market value. Furthermore, it appears that LOT was the base against which the incremental oil reduction from segregated ballasting was measured, and this involves some questionable assumptions as to the efficiency with which LOT operates in practice. Nevertheless, this conclusion is so striking as to call into question the economic rationale of the mandatory segregated ballasting provision in the convention.

The explanation for adoption of segregated ballasting at the conference (which remained the U.S. position, despite the Treasury study) can be found in enforcement. As noted earlier, a major disadvantage of LOT is that it is subject to human failures, both willful and inadvertent. Furthermore, there does not appear to be an automatic, tamper-proof, oil discharge monitoring system available, and compliance with discharge limits and LOT would depend on the alertness and motivation of the crew, but could not be easily verified. In contrast, a design change requirement such as mandatory segregated ballasting automatically solves the dirty ballast

[13] Cheng, "Is Compulsory Segregated Ballasting Needed?"

problem, and the only inspection necessary is a certification that sufficient segregated ballasting facilities are in place. Thus, a trade-off was made—a high degree of enforcement at some additional cost for tanker construction.[14] There is also the theoretical disadvantage that mandatory segregated ballasting eliminates incentive for innovation and cost reduction in pollution abatement, as, for example, the perfection of tank membranes to physically separate cargo from ballast water.

The question of instruments for controlling routine oil discharge, then, contains the classic issues in environmental control policies generally. On the one hand, mandatory design requirements may miss least-cost solutions and inhibit innovation, on the other hand, they offer greater certainty of compliance and reduce enforcement costs.

The final question for decision, after accepting segregated ballasting, was to consider whether this should be accomplished by using double bottoms. An interesting cost-effectiveness study of this question was done by the U.S. Coast Guard, with the conclusion that double bottoms were warranted. Data from this study are presented in Table 8.

The table shows the additional capital cost of segregated ballasting to be $1.6 million for a 250,000 ton tanker and the additional cost of segregated ballasting with double bottom to be $3.3 million. Single-skin segregated ballasting reduced operational outflow to 32% of the base ship using just LOT, but increases accidental outflow to 124% of the base ship. Double bottoms reduce operational outflow to 4.6% of base ship and accidental outflow to 65% of base ship.

The final line item gives the reduction in total outflow over twenty years in cubic meters per $1 million of additional capital costs. Thus, $1 million spent on single-skin segregated ballasting reduces outflow over twenty years by 740 C.M. and $1 million spent on double bottoms reduces outlfow by 1,000 C.M. On the basis of this study and IMCO background study I, prepared by the United States, the United States supported

---

[14] That additional costs of segregated ballasting were not ignored is clear from the exemption of existing ships and for tankers under 70,000 tons.

TABLE 8. COST-EFFECTIVENESS COMPARISON OF SINGLE-SKIN
AND DOUBLE-BOTTOM TANKERS (250,000 tons)[a]

	Base (comparison) ship Conventional LOT tanker (millions)	Staggered-wing segregated ballast (single-skin) (millions)	Double-bottom segregated ballast (millions)
Capital investment	$37.7	$39.3	$41.8
Increase in cost		$ 1.6	$ 3.3
% Increase in cost		4.25%	8.75%
Average annual operational out-flow	129 cubic meters	41 C.M. (32% base ship)	6 C.M. (4.6% base ship)
Average annual accidental out-flow	123 cubic meters	152 C.M. (124% base ship)	80 C.M. (65% base ship)
Average annual total outflow	252 cubic meters	193 C.M. (76% base ship)	86 C.M. (34% base ship)
Reduction in out-flow for 20 years per $million of additional cap-ital cost		740 C.M.	1,000 C.M.

[a]"Tankers with Segregated Ballast and Double Bottoms," Merchant Marine Technical Division, U.S. Coast Guard Headquarters (Oct. 16, 1972).

a provision in the convention requiring that segregated bal-lasting be accomplished in part by double bottoms. This failed to find general support and was not included in the final convention document. The reasons are the additional cost of double bottoms and the contention that in a tanker grounding incident double bottoms might actually increase oil spillage before refloating.

It is interesting to note at this point the relation of the multilateral control effort and U.S. legislation. The U.S. Ports and Waterways Safety Act of 1972 called upon the Coast Guard to establish design and construction regulations for U.S. flag vessels engaged in coastwise trade, which would include coastal shipment of oil from the Port Valdez terminal of the trans-Alaskan pipeline. A proposed regulation was issued in January 1973, which would require segregated ballasting with double bottoms for all tankers delivered after January 1, 1976 and for tankers contracted for after January 1, 1974. Thus the prospective situation of U.S. flag vessels required to use expensive double bottoms in delivering Alaskan oil, and in competition with foreign flag vessels delivering to U.S. ports with less stringent environmental safeguards, has been a source of concern.

As with the Ocean Dumping Convention, the welfare distributional consequence of the Convention on the Prevention of Pollution from Ships can be classified as domestic, external (international), intertemporal redistribution, and the question of rent. With regard to the last two classifications, the arguments and conclusions developed earlier, in the discussion of ocean dumping, also hold for pollution from ships convention. In particular, if the oceans indeed have an assimilative capacity and if global assimilative capacity in all mediums and locations is economically scarce, then the waste disposal capacity of the oceans provides an economically valuable service. Moreover, if they were under effective control the "owner" of this resource service could extract an economic rent, the amount of which would be set by the cost (financial and environmental) of alternative disposal methods. Assuming that the provisions of the conventions do not limit waste flows into the marine environment below this assimilative capacity (which would be irrational), the situation following implementation of the conventions is still one in which the putative owners are making an implicit gift to waste disposers and are foregoing rental income from their "common heritage." Care would have to be taken, of course, to distinguish between rental income to the owner of a natural resource and the extraction of monopoly profits.

The domestic distribution of costs and benefits resulting from the convention cannot be fully quantified. The major cost will be felt in petroleum transport, although Annex II costs, related to the transport of non-oil bulk liquids, will be felt in various chemical and petrochemical products. We can expect these latter to be incorporated in product prices over time and widely diffused throughout the economy, without significant concentration on one group. The cost of oil and oil products will rise as a result of the implementation of Annex I provisions. These increases may be substantial—taking the capital cost data on segregated ballasting (single-skin) and data on projected tanker construction, the additional ship-building cost between now and 1980 might be $0.6 to $1.9 billion. When converted to annual costs and adjusted for tonnage, freight rates may rise from 2 to 5%. Combining this information with data on expected oil import patterns, the annual incremental oil transport cost for the United States from segregated ballasting may fall between 10 and 77 million dollars, depending on assumptions.[15] In any event, we may expect in the long run for these costs to enter product prices, and the distribution of costs would be approximated by consumption patterns. Specifically, 58% of petroleum goes directly to transport (mainly autos), 22% for household and commercial use, and 20% for industrial users. There will also be a geographic effect—the East coast, being more heavily dependent on imported oil, will bear a disproportionate cost burden (but, as it suffers the greatest marine pollution, it will also secure a disproportionate benefit). This effect will be lessened if competition equalizes price and rent on pipelined domestic oil increase. In any event, the cost increases set against recent increases in the price of oil for other reasons are very small, and there does not seem to be a serious domestic equity issue with regard to the incremental environmental control costs.

Data on domestic beneficiaries of marine pollution abatement are scarce and incomplete. The authority on the subject, Tihansky, has estimated damages (benefits) from U.S. coastal marine pollution (abatement) for the year 1970 to be $27.5 to $65.3 million for public beach swimming, using the methodologically sound consumer surplus approach; $70.9 million for clams and oysters; near-shore fin fish at $37.5 million; and $17.4 to $34.8 million for damages to navigation

---

[15] Cheng estimates $120 million. Data presented here are taken from "Oil Tanker Pollution Control," paper in preparation by P. Cummins, R. Tollison, D. Logue, and T. Willett.

from floating debris.[16] For our purposes these data are incomplete for two reasons. First, they include damages from all sources of marine pollution, not only ocean dumping or ship-based pollution. Second, there are no estimates of other types of damages—sport fishing, direct effect on human health, other fish stocks, recreational boating, sea bird populations, and so forth. One can conclude, however, that the domestic beneficiaries of marine pollution abatement will be widely dispersed, and, in conjunction with the wide distribution of costs, there is no need for compensatory domestic policy to reestablish an equitable welfare distribution.

Internationally, one might compute the welfare distributional consequences of the convention by comparing for each country the expected reduction in environmental damages with the expected increase in transport costs. Again, the largest relative gainers will be states which depend heavily on the oceans for beneficial use and who rely least on ocean transport of petroleum and other noxious substances.

We have not attempted in this study to quantify the distribution of costs and benefits by country for methodological and data reasons. We have, however, included three tables illustrating the major interarea oil flows, the employment of tankers in various routes, and the ownership of the world's tanker fleet. Together these data provide certain presumptive evidence of the distribution of the additional costs arising from the Prevention of Pollution from Ships Convention, although we are quick to add that the data are suggestive rather than conclusive.

Table 9 presents information on total oil movements among major areas, the overwhelming majority of which moves by tanker. It can be seen from the table that the U.S. imports currently account for less than 20% of world imports. Note that U.S. imports from the Caribbean, our dominant source of

[16] D. Tihansky, "An Economic Assessment of Marine Water Pollution Damages," in *1973 Pollution Control in the Marine Industries*, ed. by T. Sullivan for International Association for Pollution Control (1973). D. Tihansky, "Recreational Welfare Losses from Water Pollution Along U.S. Coasts," *Journal of Environmental Quality* (forthcoming).

TABLE 9. INTERAREA TOTAL OIL MOVEMENTS 1973

From	To										Total exports
	U.S.A.	Canada	Other Western Hemisphere	Western Europe	Africa	South East Asia	Japan	Australia	Other Eastern Hemisphere	Destination not known [a]	
	(million tons)										
U.S.A.	–	1.5	3.0	4.8	0.2	1.3	1.7	–	–	–	12.5
Canada	67.0	–	–	–	–	–	–	–	–	–	67.01
Caribbean	131.1	25.1	6.2	17.5	0.2	0.3	0.5	–	–	6.6	187.5
Other Western Hemisphere	4.0	–	4.7	–	–	–	–	–	–	1.6	10.3
Western Europe	13.0	–	–	–	3.0	–	–	–	0.5	3.1	19.6
Middle East	40.8	16.0	47.4	513.3	26.0	65.1	215.9	13.9	38.9	11.7	989.0
North Africa	17.8	2.0	8.4	120.8	0.2	–	1.0	–	12.6	0.5	163.3
West Africa	25.2	4.4	20.3	50.3	–	–	5.4	–	0.2	–	105.8
South East Asia	11.8	–	–	0.5	–	–	54.8	2.0	–	–	69.1
U.S.S.R., E. Europe	1.8	–	7.0	48.6	3.6	0.3	2.7	–	1.0	1.8	66.8
Other Eastern Hemisphere	0.7	–	–	–	–	1.2	1.7	–	0.2	0.3	4.1
Total imports	313.2	49.0	97.0	755.8	33.2	68.2	283.7	15.9	53.4	25.6	1,695.0

Source: *BP Statistical Review of the World Oil Industry 1973.*

[a]Includes quantities in transit, transit losses, minor movements not otherwise shown, military use, etc.

supply, include Middle Eastern and Venezuelan crude that is refined and trans-shipped to U.S. ports, and thus understates the cost of oil movement to the United States. Other important oil trade routes are from the Middle East to Western Europe (513 million tons) and to Japan (216 million tons). The international pattern of oil flows is confirmed in Table 10, which shows the employment of ocean-going tankers on major routes. Specifically, 46.5% of the tanker fleet is on the Middle East–Western Europe route and 14.0% on the Middle East–Japan route. Seven percent are on the U.S.–Caribbean and U.S.–Middle East routes. Finally, Table 11 gives some information on tanker registry and ownership. Again the data should be interpreted with great caution, not least because the country of registry is often different from the nationality of ownership. In any event, it can be seen that Liberia, Norway, The United Kingdom, and Japan are the important flag states, accounting for 62% of the world's fleet, that they are almost exclusively privately owned, and that, except for

TABLE 10. EMPLOYMENT OF TANKERS 1973

Estimated proportions of World's Active ocean-going fleet on main voyages (%)

Voyages to	Voyages from					
	U.S.A.	Carib-bean	Middle East	North Africa	Others	Total
U.S.A.	3.0	3.0	4.0	1.0	2.5	13.5
Canada	–	0.5	1.5	–	0.5	2.5
Other Western Hemisphere	–	–	4.0	0.5	2.0	6.5
Western Europe, N. & W. Africa	–	1.0	46.5	3.0	3.0	53.5
E. & S. Africa, S. Asia	–	–	1.5	–	0.5	2.0
Japan	–	–	14.0	–	3.0	17.0
Other Eastern Hemisphere	–	–	4.0	–	–	4.0
U.S.S.R., E. Europe & China	–	–	1.0	–	–	1.0
Total	3.0%	4.5%	76.5%	4.5%	11.5%	100%

Source: BP Statistical Review of the World Oil Industry 1973.

TABLE 11. WORLD TANKER FLEET AT END OF 1973
(Excluding 36.8 Million D.W.T. Combined Carriers)
(2,000 D.W. Tons and Over) (by flag and ownership)

	Ownership					
Flag	Oil company	Private	Govern-ment	Other	Total 1973	Share of total 1973(%)
	(Million tons deadweight)					
Liberia	13.9	45.1	–	0.3	59.3	27
Norway	0.5	20.9	–	–	21.4	10
U.K.	18.0	9.8	0.2	–	28.0	13
Japan	3.3	23.6	–	–	26.9	12
U.S.A.	3.8	4.3	1.6	–	9.7	4
Panama	3.7	4.0	–	–	7.7	3
France	6.7	2.9	0.1	–	9.7	4
Greece	–	12.7	–	–	12.7	6
Other Western Europe	10.6	16.1	0.1	–	26.8	12
Other Western Hemi-sphere	5.0	0.4	0.3	–	5.7	3
U.S.S.R., E. Europe, & China	–	–	6.4	–	6.4	3
Other Eastern Hemi-sphere	1.9	3.7	0.1	–	5.7	3
Total	67.4	143.5	8.8	0.3	220.0	100%

Source: BP Statistical Review of the World Oil Industry 1973.

the United Kingdom, private (charter) operations are more important than oil company ownership of tanker fleets.

More generally, we draw the following conclusions concerning the relationship of international welfare distribution and the negotiation of multilateral environmental control measures. First, it does not appear that the distributional issue obstructed the negotiation of the Ocean Dumping Convention, but it probably influenced the form of the agreement, particularly the broad authority granted to national governments in issuing specific regulations. International agreement was necessary where the level of reciprocal externalities was extensive—and, indeed, led to the regional North Sea Ocean Dumping Convention. In these circumstances one would not expect individual countries to unilaterally limit dumping, subjecting their own citizens to increased costs without necessarily improving the marine environment. The United States could easily support nonspecific multilateral agreement, as our situation was one in which a significant portion of our dumping damages were internal to the country as a whole, and we would have proceeded with unilateral action in any event.

Second, there is considerable evidence that cost considerations were important in formulating the Prevention of Pollution from Ships Convention. This is true for the convention decision regarding double bottoms, setting the lower bound for segregated ballasting at 70,000 tons and establishing the data for "new" ships as those contracted for after December 31, 1975, or delivered after December 31, 1979. It is not possible to say with certainty that these decisions were taken because they were valid from a global benefit cost perspective, or because they were valid from the perspective of certain key countries. While some countries, which a priori should be most concerned with the abatement cost aspect of the convention, because of their reliance on ocean transport of oil and their strong maritime interests, supported the less expensive side of these three decisions, this was not always the case.

It is certainly possible but undemonstrated that the agreement, while improving global welfare, falls short of a more optimal outcome because the international distributional aspects are skewed and compensatory mechanisms are not in place.

Finally, we note that there may result some inadvertent welfare transfers internationally because of the unequal weight of various countries. When major maritime countries agree on pollution abatement design standards they can compel compliance of smaller countries up to their levels, regardless of the benefit-cost calculus of smaller states. Tankers will generally be constructed to meet the design standards necessary to serve major markets, and over time, as older tankers go out of service, the smaller states will have limited transport alternatives. They will be obliged to use modes of transportation that meet the specifications of the major countries. Perhaps too much should not be made of this in an environmentally united world.

APPENDIX I
OCEAN DUMPING AND PREVENTION OF POLLUTION FROM SHIPS CONVENTIONS

PREAMBLE TO THE
OCEAN DUMPING CONVENTION*

The Contracting Parties to this Convention

Recognizing that the marine environment and the living organisms which it supports are of vital importance to humanity, and all people have an interest in assuring that it is so managed that its quality and resources are not impaired;

Recognizing that the capacity of the sea to assimilate wastes and render them harmless, and its ability to regenerate natural resources, is not unlimited;

Recognizing that States have, in accordance with the Charter of the United Nations and the principles of international law, the sovereign right to exploit their own resources pursuant to their own environmental policies, and the responsibility to ensure that activities within their jurisdiction or control do not cause damage to the environment of other States or of areas beyond the limits of national jurisdiction;

Recalling Resolution 2749 (XXV) of the General Assembly of the United Nations on the principles governing the sea bed and the ocean floor and the subsoil thereof, beyond the limits of national jurisdiction;

Noting that marine pollution originates in many sources, such as dumping and discharges through the atmosphere, rivers, estuaries, outfalls and pipelines, and that it is important that States use the best practicable means to prevent such pollution and develop products and processes which will reduce the amount of harmful wastes to be disposed of;

Being convinced that international action to control the pollution of the sea by dumping can and must be taken without delay but that

*Reprinted in *International Legal Materials* no. 6 (November 1972).

106

this action should not preclude discussion of measures to control other sources of marine pollution as soon as possible and;

Wishing to improve protection of the marine environment by encouraging States with a common interest in particular geographical areas to enter into appropriate agreements supplementary to this Convention:

Have agreed as follows:

ARTICLE I

Contracting Parties shall individually and collectively promote the effective control of all sources of pollution of the marine environment, and pledge themselves especially to take all practicable steps to prevent the pollution of the sea by the dumping of waste and other matter that is liable to create hazards to human health, to harm living resources and marine life, to damage amenities or to interfere with other legitimate uses of the sea.

ARTICLE II

Contracting Parties shall, as provided for in the following Articles, take effective measures individually, according to their scientific, technical and economic capabilities, and collectively, to prevent marine pollution caused by dumping and shall harmonize their policies in this regard.

ARTICLE III

For the purposes of this Convention:

1. (a) ''Dumping'' means:
    (i) any deliberate disposal at sea of wastes or other matter from vessels, aircraft, platforms or other man-made structures at sea;
    (ii) any deliberate disposal at sea of vessels, aircraft, platforms or other man-made structures at sea;
   (b) ''Dumping'' does not include:
    (i) the disposal at sea of wastes or other matter incidental to, or derived from the normal operations of vessels, aircraft, platforms or other man-made structures at sea and their equipment, other than wastes or other matter transported by or to vessels, aircraft, platforms or other man-made structures at sea, operating for the purpose of disposal of

such matter or derived from the treatment of such wastes or other matter on such vessels, aircraft platforms or structures.

(ii) placement of matter for a purpose other than the mere disposal thereof, provided that such placement is not contrary to the aims of this convention.

(c) The disposal of wastes or other matter directly arising from, or related to the exploration, exploitation and associated off-shore processing of seabed mineral resources will not be covered by the provisions of this Convention.

2. "Vessels and aircraft" means waterborne or airborne craft of any type whatsoever. This expression includes air cushioned craft and floating craft, whether self-propelled or not.

3. "Sea" means all marine waters other than the internal waters of States.

4. "Wastes or other matter" means material and substance of any kind, form or description.

5. "Special permit" means permission granted specifically on application in advance and in accordance with Annex II and Annex III.

6. "General permit" means permission granted in advance and in accordance with Annex III.

7. "The Organisation" means the organisation designated by the Contracting Parties in accordance with Article XIV2.

ARTICLE IV

1. In accordance with the provisions of this Convention, Contracting Parties shall prohibit the dumping of any wastes or other matter in whatever form or condition except as otherwise specified below:

a. The dumping of wastes or other matter listed in Annex I is prohibited;

b. The dumping of wastes or other matter listed in Annex II requires a prior special permit;

c. The dumping of all other wastes or matter requires a prior general permit.

2. Any permit shall be issued only after careful consideration of all the factors set forth in Annex III, including prior studies of the characteristics of the dumping site, as set forth in Sections B and C of that Annex.

3. No provision of this Convention is to be interpreted as preventing a Contracting Party from prohibiting, insofar as that Party is concerned, the dumping of wastes or other mattr not mentioned in Annex I. That Party shall notify such measures to the Organisation.

ARTICLE V

1. The provisions of Article IV shall not apply when it is necessary to secure the safety of human life or of vessels, aircraft, platforms or other man-made structures at sea in cases of force majeure caused by stress of weather, or in any case which constitutes a danger to human life or a real threat to vessels, aircraft, platforms or other man-made structures at sea, if dumping appears to be the only way of averting the threat and if there is every probability that the damage consequent upon such dumping will be less than would otherwise occur. Such dumping shall be so conducted as to minimise the likelihood of damage to human or marine life and shall be reported forthwith to the Organisation.

2. A Contracting Party may issue a special permit as an exception to Article IV1a, in emergencies, posing unacceptable risk relating to human health and admitting no other feasible solution. Before doing so the Party shall consult any other country or countries that are likely to be affected and the Organisation which, after consulting other Parties, and international organisations as appropriate, shall, in accordance with Article XIV promptly recommend to the Party the most appropriate procedures to adopt. The Party shall follow these recommendations to the maximum extent feasible consistent with the time within which action must be taken and with the general obligation to avoid damage to the marine environment and shall inform the Organisation of the action it takes. The Parties pledge themselves to assist one another in such situations.

3. Any Contracting Party may waive its rights under paragraph 2 at the time of, or subsequent to ratification of, or accession to this Convention.

ARTICLE VI

1. Each Contracting Party shall designate an appropriate authority or authorities to:
   a. issue special permits which shall be required prior to, and for, the dumping of matter listed in Annex II and in the circumstances provided for in Article V2;

    b. issue general permits which shall be required prior to and for the dumping of all other matter;

    c. keep records of the nature and quantities of all matter permitted to be dumped and the location, time and method of dumping;

    d. monitor individually, or in collaboration with other Parties and competent international organisations, the condition of the seas for the purposes of this Convention.

2. The appropriate authority or authorities of a Contracting Party shall issue prior special or general permits in accordance with paragraph 1 in respect of matter intended for dumping:

    a. loaded in its territory;

    b. loaded by a vessel or aircraft registered in its territory or flying its flag, when the loading occurs in the territory of a State not party to this Convention.

3. In issuing permits under sub-paragraphs 1a and b above, the appropriate authority or authorities shall comply with Annex III, together with such additional criteria, measures and requirements as they may consider relevant.

4. Each Contracting Party, directly or through a Secretariat established under a regional agreement, shall report to the Organisation, and where appropriate to other Parties, the information specified in sub-paragraphs c and d of paragraph 1 above, and the criteria, measures and requirements it adopts in accordance with paragraph 3 above. The procedure to be followed and the nature of such reports shall be agreed by the Parties in consultation.

ARTICLE VII

1. Each Contracting Party shall apply the measures required to implement the present convention to all:

    a. vessels and aircraft registered in its territory or flying its flag;

    b. vessels and aircraft loading in its territory or territorial seas matter which is to be dumped;

    c. vessels and aircraft and fixed or floating platforms under its jurisdiction believed to be engaged in dumping.

2. Each Party shall take in its territory appropriate measures to prevent and punish conduct in contravention of the provisions of this Convention.

3. The Parties agree to co-operate in the development of procedures for the effective application of this Convention particularly on the high seas, including procedures for the reporting of vessels and aircraft observed dumping in contravention of the Convention.

4. This Convention shall not apply to those vessels and aircraft entitled to sovereign immunity under international law. However, each party shall ensure by the adoption of appropriate measures that such vessels and aircraft owned or operated by it act in a manner consistent with the object and purpose of this Convention, and shall inform the Organisation accordingly.

5. Nothing in this Convention shall affect the right of each Party to adopt other measures, in accordance with the principles of international law, to prevent dumping at sea.

ARTICLE VIII

In order to further the objectives of this Convention, the Contracting Parties with common interests to protect in the marine environment in a given geographical area shall endeavour, taking into account characteristic regional features, to enter into regional agreements consistent with this Convention for the prevention of pollution, especially by dumping. The Contracting Parties to the present Convention shall endeavor to act consistently with the objectives and provisions of such regional agreements, which shall be notified to them by the Organisation. Contracting Parties shall seek to co-operate with the Parties to regional agreements in order to develop harmonized procedures to be followed by Contracting Parties to the different conventions concerned. Special attention shall be given to co-operation in the field of monitoring and scientific research.

ARTICLE IX

The Contracting Parties shall promote, through collaboration within the Organization and other international bodies, support for those Parties which request it for:
  a. the training of scientific and technical personnel;
  b. the supply of necessary equipment and facilities for research and monitoring;
  c. the disposal and treatment of waste and other measures to prevent or mitigate pollution caused by dumping; preferably

within the countries concerned, so furthering the aims and purposes of this Convention.

ARTICLE X

In accordance with the principles of international law regarding state responsibility for damage to the environment of other States or to any other area of the environment, caused by dumping of wastes and other matter of all kinds, the Contracting Parties undertake to develop procedures for the assessment of liability and the settlement of disputes regarding dumping.

ARTICLE XI

The Contracting Parties shall at their first consultative meeting consider procedures for the settlement of disputes concerning the interpretation and application of this Convention.

ARTICLE XII

The Contracting Parties pledge themselves to promote, within the competent specialized agencies and other international bodies, measures to protect the marine environment against pollution caused by:

(a) hydrocarbons, including oil, and their wastes;
(b) other noxious or hazardous matter transported by vessels for purposes other than dumping;
(c) wastes generated in the course of operation of vessels, aircraft, platforms and other man-made structures at sea;
(d) radioactive pollutants from all sources, including vessels;
(e) agents of chemical and biological warfare;
(f) wastes or other matter directly arising from, or related to the exploration, exploitation and associated off-shore processing of seabed mineral resources.

The Parties will also promote, within the appropriate international organization, the codification of signals to be used by vessels engaged in dumping.

ARTICLE XIII

Nothing in this Convention shall prejudice the codification and development of the law of the sea by the United Nations Conference on the Law of the Sea convened pursuant to Resolution 2750C (XXV) of the General Assembly of the United Nations nor the present or future claims and legal views of any State concerning the law of the sea and the nature and extent of coastal and flag state jurisdiction. The Contracting Parties agree to consult at a meeting to be convened by the Organisation after the Law of the Sea Conference, and in any case not later than 1976, with a view to defining the nature and extent of the right and the responsibility of a coastal state to apply the Convention in a zone adjacent to its coast.

ARTICLE XIV

1. The Government of the United Kingdom of Great Britain and Northern Ireland as a depositary shall call a meeting of the Contracting Parties not later than three months after the entry into force of this Convention to decide on organisational matters.

2. The Contracting Parties shall designate a competent Organisation existing at the time of that meeting to be responsible for secretariat duties in relation to this Convention. Any Party to this Convention not being a member of this Organisation shall make an appropriate contribution to the expenses incurred by the Organisation in performing these duties.

3. The Secretariat duties of the Organisation shall include:
   a. the convening of consultative meetings of the Contracting Parties not less frequently than once every two years and of special meetings of the Parties at any time on the request of two-thirds of the Parties;
   b. preparing and assisting, in consultation with the Contracting Parties and appropriate International Organisations, in the development and implementation of procedures referred to in sub-paragraph 4e of this Article.
   c. considering enquiries by, and information from the Contracting Parties, consulting with them and with the appropriate International Organisations, and providing recommendations to the Parties on questions related to, but not specifically covered by the Convention.
   d. conveying to the Parties concerned all notifications received by the Organisations in accordance with Articles IV 3, V 1 and 2, VI 4, XIII, XX and XXI.

Prior to the designation of the Organisation these functions shall, as necessary, be performed by the depositary, who for this purpose shall be the Government of the United Kingdom of Great Britain and Northern Ireland.

4. Consultative or special meetings of the Contracting Parties shall keep under continuing review the implementation of this Convention and may, inter alia:

   a. review and adopt amendments to this Convention and its Annexes in accordance with Article XV;
   b. invite the appropriate scientific body or bodies to collaborate with and to advise the Parties or the Organisation on any scientific or technical aspect relevant to this Convention, including particularly the content of the Annexes;
   c. receive and consider reports made pursuant to Article VI 4;
   d. promote co-operation with and between regional organisations concerned with the prevention of marine pollution;
   e. develop or adopt, in consultation with appropriate International Organisations, procedures referred to in Article V 2, including basic criteria for determining exceptional and emergency situations, and procedures for consultative advice and the safe disposal of matter in such circumstances, including the designation of appropriate dumping areas, and recommend accordingly;
   f. consider any additional action that may be required.

5. The Contracting Parties at their first consultative meeting shall establish rules of procedure as necessary.

ARTICLE XV

1.a. At meetings of the Contracting Parties called in accordance with Article XIV amendments to this Convention may be adopted by a two-thirds majority of those present. An amendment shall enter into force for the Parties which have accepted it on the sixtieth day after two-thirds of the Parties shall have deposited an instrument of acceptance of the amendment with the Organisation. Thereafter the amendment shall enter into force for any other Party 30 days after that Party deposits its instrument of acceptance of the amendment.

1.b. The Organisation shall inform all Contracting Parties of any requests made for a special meeting under Article XIV and of any amendments adopted at meetings of the Parties and of the date on which each such amendment enters into force for each Party.

2. Amendments to the Annexes will be based on scientific or technical considerations. Amendments to the Annexes approved by a two-thirds majority of those present at a meeting called in accordance with Article XIV shall enter into force for each Contracting Party immediately on notification of its acceptance to the Organisation and 100 days after approval by the meeting for all other Parties except for those which before the end of the 100 days make a declaration that they are not able to accept the amendment at that time. Parties should endeavour to signify their acceptance of an amendment to the Organisation as soon as possible after approval at a meeting. A Party may at any time substitute an acceptance for a previous declaration of objection and the amendment previously objected to shall thereupon enter into force for that Party.

3. An acceptance or declaration of objection under this Article shall be made by the deposit of an instrument with the Organisation. The Organisation shall notify all Contracting Parties of the receipt of such instruments.

4. Prior to the designation of the Organisation, the Secretarial functions herein attributed to it, shall be performed temporarily by the Government of the United Kingdom of Great Britain and Northern Ireland, as one of the depositaries of this Convention.

ARTICLE XVI

This Convention shall be open for signature by any State at London, Mexico City, Moscow and Washington from 29 December 1972 until 31 December 1973.

ARTICLE XVII

This Convention shall be subject to ratification. The instruments of ratification shall be deposited with the Governments of Mexico, Union of Soviet Socialist Republics, United Kingdom of Great Britain and Northern Ireland, and the United States of America.

ARTICLE XVIII

After 31 December 1973, this Convention shall be open for accession by any State. The instruments of accession shall be deposited with the Governments of Mexico, Union of Soviet Socialist Republics,

United Kingdom of Great Britain and Northern Ireland, and the United States of America.

ARTICLE XIX

1. This Convention shall enter into force on the thirtieth day following the date of deposit of the fifteenth instrument of ratification or accession.

2. For each Contracting Party ratifying or acceding to the Convention after the deposit of the fifteenth instrument of ratification or accession.

2. For each Contracting Party ratifying or acceding to the Convention after the deposit of the fifteenth instrument of ratification or accession, the Convention shall enter into force on the thirtieth day after deposit by such Party of its instrument of ratification or accession.

ARTICLE XX

The depositaries shall inform Contracting Parties:
  a. of signatures to this Convention and of the deposit of instruments of ratification, accession or withdrawal, in accordance with Articles XVI, XVII, XVIII and XXI and
  b. of the date on which this Convention will enter into force, in accordance with Article XIX.

ARTICLE XXI

Any Contracting Party may withdraw from this Convention by giving six months' notice in writing to a depositary, which shall promptly inform all Parties of such notice.

ARTICLE XXII

The original of this Convention of which the English, French, Russian and Spanish texts are equally authentic, shall be deposited with the Governments of Mexico, the Union of Soviet Socialist Republics, the United Kingdom of Great Britain and Northern Ireland and the United States of America who shall send certified copies thereof to all States.

IN WITNESS WHEREOF the undersigned Plenipotentiaries, being duly authorised thereto by their respective Governments have signed the present Convention.

DONE at . . . . . . this . . . . . . day of . . . . 1972.

ANNEX I

1. Organohalogen compounds.
2. Mercury and mercury compounds.
3. Cadmium and cadmium compounds.
4. Persistent plastics and other persistent synthetic materials, for example, netting and ropes, which may float or may remain in suspension in the sea in such a manner as to interfere materially with fishing, navigation or other legitimate uses of the sea.
5. Crude oil, fuel oil, heavy diesel oil, and lubricating oils, hydraulic fluids, and any mixtures containing any of these, taken on board for the purpose of dumping.
6. High-level radioactive wastes or other high-level radioactive matter, defined on public health, biological or other grounds, by the competent international body in this field, at present the International Atomic Energy Agency, as unsuitable for dumping at sea.
7. Materials in whatever form (e.g., solids, liquids, semi-liquids, gases or in a living state) produced for biological and chemical warfare.
8. The preceding paragraphs of this Annex do not apply to substances which are rapidly rendered harmless by physical, chemical or biological processes in the sea provided they do not:
    (i) make edible marine organisms unpalatable, or
    (ii) endanger human health or that of domestic animals.
The consultative procedure provided for under Article XIV should be followed by a Party if there is doubt about the harmlessness of the substances.
9. This Annex does not apply to wastes or other materials (e.g., sewage sludges and dredged spoils) containing the matters referred to in paragraphs 1–5 above as trace contaminants. Such wastes shall be subject to the provisions of Annexes II and III as appropriate.

ANNEX II

The following substances and materials requiring special care are listed for the purposes of Article VI 1a.

A. Wastes containing significant amounts of the matters listed below:

arsenic
lead
copper
zinc
} and their compounds

organosilicon compounds
cyanides
fluorides
pesticides and their by-products not covered in Annex I.

B. In the issue of permits for the dumping of large quantities of acids and alkalis, consideration shall be given to the possible presence in such wastes of the substances listed in paragraph A and to the following additional substances:

beryllium
chromium
nickel
vanadium
} and their compounds

C. Containers, scrap metal and other bulky wastes liable to sink to the sea bottom which may present a serious obstacle to fishing or navigation.

D. Radioactive wastes or other radioactive matter not included in Annex I. In the issue of permits for the dumping of this matter, the Contracting Parties should take full account of the recommendations of the competent international body in this field, at present the International Atomic Energy Agency.

ANNEX III

Provisions to be considered in establishing criteria governing the issue of permits for the dumping of matter at sea, taking into account Article IV 2 include:

A. Characteristics and Composition of the Matter

1. Total amount and average composition of matter dumped (e.g., per year).
2. Form, e.g., solid, sludge, liquid, or gaseous.
3. Properties: physical (e.g., solubility and density), chemical and biochemical (e.g., oxygen demand, nutrients) and biological (e.g., presence of viruses, bacteria, yeasts, parasites).
4. Toxicity.
5. Persistence: physical, chemical and biological.
6. Accumulation and biotransformation in biological materials or sediments.
7. Susceptibility to physical, chemical and biochemical changes and interaction in the aquatic environment with other dissolved organic and inorganic materials.
8. Probability of production of taints or other changes reducing marketability of resources (fish, shellfish, etc).

B. Characteristics of Dumping Site and Method of Deposit

1. Location (e.g., co-ordinates of the dumping area, depth and distance from the coast), location in relation to other areas (e.g., amenity areas, spawning, nursery and fishing areas and exploitable resources).
2. Rate of disposal per specific period (e.g., quantity per day, per week, per month).
3. Methods of packaging and containment, if any.
4. Initial dilution achieved by proposed method of release.
5. Dispersal characteristics (e.g., effects of currents, tides and wind on horizontal transport and vertical mixing).
6. Water characteristics (e.g., temperature, pH, salinity, stratification, oxygen indices of pollution—dissolved oxygen (DO), chemical oxygen demand (COD), biochemical oxygen demand (BOD)—nitrogen present in organic and mineral form including ammonia, suspended matter, other nutrients and productivity).
7. Bottom characteristics (e.g., topography, geochemical

and geological characteristics and biological productivity).

8. Existence and effects of other dumpings which have been made in the dumping area (e.g., heavy metal background reading and organic carbon content).

9. In issuing a permit for dumping, Contracting Parties should consider whether an adequate scientific basis exists for assessing the consequences of such dumping, as outlined in this Annex, taking into account seasonal variations.

C. General Considerations and Conditions

1. Possible effects on amenities (e.g., presence of floating or stranded material, turbidity, objectionable odour, discolouration and foaming).

2. Possible effects on marine life, fish and shellfish culture, fish stocks and fisheries, seaweed harvesting and culture.

3. Possible effects on other uses of the sea (e.g., impairment of water quality for industrial use, underwater corrosion of structures, interference with ship operations from floating materials, interference with fishing or navigation through deposit of waste or solid objects on the sea floor and protection of areas of special importance for scientific or conservation purposes).

4. The practical availability of alternative land based methods of treatment, disposal or elimination, or of treatment to render the matter less harmful for dumping at sea.

Comparison of Certain Major Features of International Conventions for Prevention of Pollution from Ships*

	1954 (as ammended in 1962)	1973
Applicability as regards carriage of oil	1. Seagoing tankers over 150 gross tons. 2. Other seagoing ships over 500 gross tons.	1. All tankers over 150 gross tons. 2. All other ships over 400 gross tons including novel craft and fixed and floating platforms.
Dispute settlement	1. Referred to International Court of Justice unless all parties agree to arbitration.	1. Compulsory arbitration by specially formed tribunals upon application of any party to dispute.
Amendment procedure	1. Effective only upon specific acceptance via IMCO Assembly and Contracting States.	1. Speedier method for Annexes and appendices via IMCO Committee and tacit acceptance procedures
Survey and Certification	1. No comparable provision.	1. Survey at 5-year intervals and at intermediate (mid-period) intervals. 2. Equipment must be approved by Administration (monitors, filters, separators, interface detectors). 3. Administration issues Certificate attesting to compliance by its ships, which certificate shall be accepted except when there are clear grounds to believe the ship is not in compliance.

* Appendix from "The Impact of the 1973 IMCO Convention on the Maritime Industry," by W. M. Benkert and D. H. Williams, *Marine Technology* (January 1974), published by The Society of Naval Architects and Marine Engineers; included herein by permission of the aforementioned Society.

Continued

Definition of Oil	1. Limited to crude, fuel, heavy diesel, and lubricating oils. 2. Does not include bilge slops and fuel and lube oil purification residues.	1. Includes all petroleum oils except petrochemicals (which are regulated by Annex 11).
Discharge criteria in Prohibited Zones (this term does not appear in the 1973 Convention which uses a distance-from-land criterion)	1. Prohibits discharges by all ships in concentration in excess of 100 parts per million within the prohibited zones. 2. Prohibited zone generally 50 miles or greater from nearest land for tankers. Prohibited zone applies to other ships unless proceeding to a port not provided with adequate reception facilities.	1. Prohibits discharges which leave visible traces unless it can be established by installed instruments that the concentration discharged was less than 15 parts per million. 2. For tanker cargo slops, discharge is prohibited within 50 miles from nearest land. For other ships' slops, and other tanker slops, discharge is prohibited within 12 miles from the nearest land.
Discharge criteria outside the Prohibited Zones	1. No restriction on discharges from a ship less than 20,000 gross tons. Vessels over 20,000 gross tons are limited to discharges whose concentrations are 100 parts per million or less, unless when, in the opinion of the master, circumstances make it unreasonable or impractical to retain the higher-concentrated slops on board.	1. Tankers must meet all the following conditions: *a.* ship is proceeding enroute. *b.* discharge is limited to 60 liters per mile instantaneous rate. *c.* total quantity discharged is limited to 1/15,000 of cargo last carried for existing tankers and 1/30,000 of cargo last carried for new tankers. *d.* tanker bilges, except pump rooms, shall be treated the same as other ships. 2. Other ships must meet all of the following conditions: *a.* ship proceeding enroute.

		b. oil content of the effluent must not exceed 100 parts per million.
Enforcement mechanism	1. No comparable provision.	1. Requires that the monitoring and control system be in operation and a permanent record made anytime oily effluent is being discharged, except for clean or segregated ballast.
Construction and Equipment Requirements to control operational discharges of oily mixtures.	1. No comparable provision.	1. Segregated ballast is mandatory for new tankers of 70,000 deadweight tons and greater, and is optional for tankers of less than 70,000 deadweight tons. Note that "new" tankers are defined by calendar dates and are therefore not dependent upon entry into force of this Convention. 2. Retention of Oil on Board (LOT) is mandatory for all tankers. 3. Mandatory installation of effluent monitor and control system, provision of slop tanks, and provision of oil/water interface detectors. Effluent must comply with discharge criteria or be transferred to reception facility. 4. Other ships require sludge tank installations, oil-water separators and/or filters dependent upon ship size.
Reception facilities	1. Provision to promote according to need of ships using ports.	1. Expanded provision to undertake to ensure availability and adequacy at oil loading ports, repair ports, and at other ports according to the needs of ships.

Oil Record Book	1. Establishes basic requirement to provide oil record book and the specific operations requiring entries.	1. Expands requirements to provide entries for more specific operations and in greater detail to aid in enforcement.
Construction Requirements to limit the amount of oil discharge in case of accidents.	1. No comparable provision.	1. Establishes damage assumptions and methods of calculation of the amount of hypothetical oil outflow for tankers. 2. Establishes tank arrangement and size limitations for the cargo tanks of tankers. 3. Establishes subdivision and damage stability criteria to be applied to tankers to increase survivability in the event of accident.
Additional annexes for substances other than oil. Annex II is mandatory and annexes III, IV, and V may be adopted at the option of Contracting States.	1. No comparable provision.	1. Annex II details mandatory requirements for construction features and discharge criteria for ships carrying liquid noxious substances in bulk. 2. Annex III contains regulations for the prevention of pollution by harmful substances carried at sea in packaged form, or in freight containers, portable tanks, or road and rail tank cars. 3. Annex IV contains regulations for the prevention of pollution sewage from ships. 4. Annex V contains regulations for the prevention of pollution by garbage from ships.

SELECTED BIBLIOGRAPHY

Benkert, W., and Williams, D. "The Impact of the 1973 IMCO Convention on the Maritime Industry." *Marine Technology* (January 1974).

Calabresi, G. "Transactions Costs, Resource Allocation, and Liability Rules," in Dorfman and Dorfman, eds., *Economics of the Environment*. New York: Norton, 1972.

Charter, D., and Porricelli, J. "Quantitative Estime of Petroleum to the Oceans," in, Council on Environmental Quality, *Ocean Dumping, a National Policy*. Washington, D.C.: U.S. Government Printing Office, 1970.

Cheng, Hang-Shen. "Is Compulsory Segregated Ballasting Needed and Justified for Reducing Pollution of the Sea?" U.S. Treasury, mimeo., 1973.

Christy, F. "Fisheries: Common Property, Open Access, and the Common Heritage," in *Pacem in Maribus, Vol. II*. Malta: Royal University of Malta Press, 1971.

Coase, R. "The Problem of Social Cost," in, Dorfman and Dorfman, eds., *Economics of the Environment*. New York: Norton, 1972.

Council on Environmental Quality (CEQ). *Second Annual Report (1971)*, Washington, D.C.: U.S. Government Printing Office, 1971.

_____, *Fourth Annual Report (1973)*. Washington, D.C.: U.S. Government Printing Office, 1973.

Dales, J. "Land, Water and Ownership," in, Dorfman and Dorfman, eds., *Economics of the Environment*. New York: Norton, 1972.

Demsetz, H. "Toward a Theory of Property Rights." *American Economic Association Papers and Proceedings* (May 1967).

Food and Agriculture Organization (FAO). "Report on Regulatory Fisheries Bodies." *Fisheries Circular No. 138*. Rome: Food and Agriculture Organization, 1972.

Goldman, M. "The Convergence of Environmental Disruption." *Science* (October 2, 1972).

Gordon, H. C. "The Economic Theory of a Common Property Resource: The Fishery." *Journal of Political Economy* (April 1954).

Hardin, G. "The Tragedy of the Commons." *Science* (December 13, 1968).

Hardy, M. "International Control of Marine Pollution." *Natural Resources Journal* (April 1971).

Hargrove, J. L., ed. *Law, Institutions and the Global Environment.* Dobbs Ferry, N.Y.: Oceana, 1972.

———. *Testimony at the Hearings on S. 1067, S. 1070, and S. 1351 Before the Subcommittee on Oceans and Atmosphere of the Senate Committee on Commerce,* Washington, D.C.: U.S. Government Printing Office, 1973.

International Maritime Consultative Organization (IMCO). *Report of Study No. VI. The Environmental and Financial Consequences of Oil Pollution.* U.K. Dept. of Trade and Industry, 1973.

Joint Group of Experts on the Scientific Aspects of Marine Pollution (GESAMP). *Hearings on the 1973 IMCO Conference on Marine Pollution from Ships Before Senate Committee on Commerce Report.* Washington, D.C.: U.S. Government Printing Office, 1973.

Kneese, A., and Bower, B. "Standards, Charges and Equity," in *Managing Water Quality: Economics, Technology, Institutions.* Baltimore: Johns Hopkins University Press, 1968.

Krier, J., and Montgomery, W. D. "Resource Allocation, Information Cost and the Form of Government Intervention." *Natural Resources Journal* (January 1973).

Legault, L. H. J. "The Freedom of the Seas: License to Pollute?" *University of Toronto Law Journal,* no. 2 (1971).

Mishan, E. "The Postwar Literature on Externalities: An Interpretative Essay." *Journal of Economic Literature* (March 1971).

Ogilvie, P. "Ocean Dumping and the EPA," unpublished, May 1974.

Pearson, C. "Control of Ocean Dumping." *SAIS Review* (Fall 1972).

———. "Extracting Rent from Ocean Resources: Discussion of a Neglected Source," *Journal of Ocean Development and Law* (Summer 1973).

Ross, W. *Oil Pollution as an International Problem.* Victoria, B.C.: University of Victoria, 1973.

Scott, A. "The Economics of International Transmission of Pollution," in *Problems of Environmental Economics.* Paris: OECD, 1971.

Shinn, Robert. *The International Politics of Marine Pollution Control.* New York: Praeger, 1974.

Swan, P. "International and National Approaches to Oil Pollution Responsibility: An Emerging Regime for a Global Problem." *Oregon Law Review* (Spring 1971).

Sweeney, J. "Private Damage from Oil Spills in a Marine Environment," in, The Institute on Man and Science, *Assessing the Social Impacts of Oil Spills.* Ransselaerville, N.Y.: The Institute on Man and Science, 1973.

Thacher, P. "Assessment and Control of Marine Pollution: The Stockholm Conference and their Efficacy." *Stanford Journal of International Studies* (Spring 1973).

Tihansky, D. "An Economic Assessment of Marine Water Pollution Damages," in, International Association for Pollution Control, *1973 Pollution Control in the Marine Industries.* Washington, D.C.: 1973.

_____. "Recreational Welfare Losses from Water Pollution Along U.S. Coasts." *Journal of Environmental Quality* (forthcoming).

U.S. Coast Guard. "Tankers with Segregated Ballast and Double Bottoms," mimeo. by Merchant Marine Technical Division, Washington, D.C., October 16, 1972.

U.S. Congress. *Hearings on the 1973 IMCO Conference Before the Senate Committee on Commerce (November 1973).* Washington, D.C.: U.S. Government Printing Office.

_____. *Hearings on H.R. 5450 Before the Subcommittee on Fisheries and Wildlife Conservation and the Environment and the Subcommittee on Oceanography of the House Committee on Merchant Marine and Fisheries (1973).* Washington, D.C.: U.S. Government Printing Office.

Library of Congress Cataloging in Publication Data

Pearson, Charles S.
    International marine environment policy.

    (Studies in international affairs; no. 25)
    Bibliograpy: pp. 125–27.
    1.   Marine pollution—Law and legislation.
    2.   Environmental law, International. I. Title.
II. Series: Washington Center of Foreign Policy
Research. Studies in international affairs;
no. 25.
Law   341.7'65   74–24793
ISBN 0–8018–1712–9
ISBN 0–8018–1713–7 pbk.